BIOETHICS AND HIGH-TECH MEDICINE

VICTORIA SHERROW

BIOETHICS AND HIGH-TECH MEDICINE

TWENTY-FIRST CENTURY BOOKS
A DIVISION OF HENRY HOLT AND COMPANY   NEW YORK

Twenty-First Century Books
A Division of Henry Holt and Company, Inc.
115 West 18th Street
New York, NY 10011

Henry Holt® and colophon are trademarks of
Henry Holt and Company, Inc.
Publishers since 1866

Published in Canada by Fitzhenry & Whiteside Ltd.
195 Allstate Parkway, Markham, Ontario L3R 4T8

Library of Congress Cataloging-in-Publication Data
Sherrow, Victoria.
Bioethics and high-tech medicine/Victoria Sherrow.—1st ed.
p. cm.
Summary: Discusses biomedical technologies and their consequences
including the ethical dilemmas that arise.
1. Medical ethics—Juvenile literature. [1. Medical ethics.] I. Title.
R724.S477 1996   95-34222
174'.2—dc20   CIP
                                                       AC
ISBN 0-8050-3832-9
First Edition 1996

174.2
S
c. 1

DESIGNED BY KATE NICHOLS

Printed in the United States of America
All first editions are printed on acid-free paper ∞.
10 9 8 7 6 5 4 3 2 1

CONTENTS

ONE

Uncharted Territory

IT HAS BEEN SAID THAT WE LIVE IN AN AGE OF SCIEN-
tific and medical miracles. Since the mid-1900s, an explosion of
scientific knowledge has made it possible to create new life-forms
and to decide, in many cases, who shall be born, who shall live,
and who shall die. As the twenty-first century approaches, new
medical technology has given humans unprecedented control over
life and death.

Scientific breakthroughs bring not only triumph over disease
and disability but also bring complex choices and ethical dilemmas.
Perhaps you or someone you know has inherited a health problem—sickle-cell anemia, Down syndrome, cystic fibrosis. Maybe
your family has a history of breast cancer, or elderly members suffer from Alzheimer's disease. You may know somebody who needs
an organ transplant or has tried without success to conceive a
child.

These situations involve biomedical ethics, often shortened to
bioethics. This subject deals with the moral and social aspects of
practices and developments in medicine and science.[1] It involves

choices, often difficult ones. Ethics have concerned humankind for thousands of years. As author Helge Kuhse says, "Wherever people are living together, there is ethics; conduct is classified as 'right' or 'wrong'; standards are set."[2] Joseph Fletcher says that ethics embodies two elements: "the values with which people approach their choices and decisions, and the logic (or lack of it) with which they relate their values to their decisions."[3] By going through this kind of thinking process, we decide what we believe is the right thing to do.

The ways in which bioethical dilemmas are handled may differ from place to place. The framework for making such decisions includes patients and their religious and moral beliefs; parents or other family members; the social community, which exercises approval or disapproval about how people conduct themselves; federal and state laws; physicians; and the hospital, which has written or informal rules, standards, and procedures.

Hospital ethics committees typically include physicians, other health care professionals, and religious, legal, and ethical experts. They discuss the issues and make recommendations in particular cases. Critics of committee-made decisions point out that these people do not have to live with the consequences as patients, parents, and families do.

In making bioethical decisions, individuals may consider their personal opinions, religious and ethical beliefs, and any laws that apply to a given situation. There may be no well-defined standards that fit the situation. Searching for answers in an individual case or in regard to larger health issues, we may refer to these six general principles:

- Autonomy: being free to make decisions involving one's own or a family member's health and well-being
- Beneficence: doing the right thing; providing or promoting well-being and preventing harm
- Justice: being fair

- Nonmaleficence: doing no harm; acting with no harmful or selfish motives toward another person or society
- Veracity: telling the truth
- Fidelity: keeping all contracts and promises.[4]

As we examine various bioethical dilemmas, we can see how these principles come into play. In certain areas, some factors count more than others—for example, in medical research, veracity and nonmaleficence are key concerns; with transplants, questions of justice may receive more weight.

The following situations show dilemmas that can arise:

Huntington's disease is a neurological illness that strikes people after age thirty-five, causing devastating physical and mental symptoms—muscle spasms, convulsions, rages, paranoia, delusions—followed by early death. Children of Huntington's victims have a 50 percent chance of inheriting the gene that causes the disease. In the past, people had to wait until symptoms appeared in midlife, after they had already given birth to their own children, to find out if they had Huntington's. By 1993, scientists had located the defective gene that causes Huntington's and developed a screening test that can determine its presence. New screening tests are also available for numerous conditions, including breast and colon cancer, cystic fibrosis, and muscular dystrophy.

What are the pros and cons of taking such tests and learning about one's fate? Would you want to know? Would you have your children tested? Society has an interest in lowering health care costs, and prevention and early treatment often cost less. This has led to debates over the possibility of mandatory screening for certain diseases and to concern that laws could be passed banning people with certain diseases from having children. In the meantime, some bioethicists say that it is not proper even to devise tests for diseases like Huntington's that have no real treatment or cure.

■

In 1994, scientists announced promising results from an experiment to reverse an inherited disease in which patients lack a gene that helps the body to absorb cholesterol. Dangerously high levels of cholesterol accumulate in their blood and can clog their arteries, causing heart attacks and other problems at a young age. In its severe form, familial hypercholesterolemia, the disease strikes about one in one million Americans. Scientists inserted copies of the missing gene in a thirty-year-old woman with the disease. They removed 15 percent of her liver and cultured the tissues so that cells could be grown in the laboratory. After supplying these cells with the missing gene, they reinserted the cells into the patient's liver. Some resettled and began producing the cholesterol receptor.

Gene technology has led to promising new treatments for disease and has enhanced the quality of life for many people. It also makes it possible to alter human traits. Should such technology be reserved for disease-related conditions, or should we also use it to alter or "enhance" human beings? What might be the consequences of using technology to produce babies with traits their parents deem most desirable? Critics worry about the use of such techniques on sperm and egg cells, since that means passing on the changed traits to future generations.

■

A child has only one kidney, which is failing. Her rare tissue type makes it unlikely that a donor can ever be found. The parents decide to have another child and use one of its kidneys for the transplant. Can we presume the child would consent to donate its organs? Is it ethical to reproduce a child for this purpose?

These are but a few of the bioethical dilemmas we now face. Such dilemmas increase in number and complexity as the frontiers of health care broaden each year.

RISING EXPECTATIONS FOR
HEALTH CARE

In 1982, a presidential commission defined health care as "the prevention of death and disability, the relief of pain and suffering, the restoration of functioning."[5] Centuries ago, medicine had far less to offer people. Death often came at an earlier age, frequently as a result of infectious diseases that were then incurable. Modern sanitation, antiseptics, effective vaccines, antibiotics, and diagnostic and surgical techniques changed the focus of medicine from caring for patients to curing them. As science tackled one problem after another, people formed increasingly higher expectations. It seemed to be only a matter of time before all human maladies would be conquered.

Today, more people use more health care services than at any other time in history. In 1982, the President's Commission for the Study of Ethical Problems in Medicine and Biomedical and Behavioral Research reported that three out of ten Americans or a member of their immediate family had experienced a *life-threatening* illness or medical condition.[6]

Medical intervention can take place throughout the life cycle, even before birth, as when people use reproductive technology. Tiny, very premature newborns can be kept alive with machines. So can severely injured people, elderly people with multiple health problems, and those whose organs have failed. Most patients expect to receive any treatment that can possibly help them. We strive for health and seek to avoid disease, disability, and death, often with the help of medical technology.

Biotechnology is often described as a double-edged sword, bringing not only improvements in our lives but personal and global problems. At times, scientific knowledge has been applied quickly, without considering all the implications. For example, the use of modern chemicals and fuels has brought pollution and other environmental problems. In the early days of nuclear research, lab workers developed cancer because the risks of handling radioactive materials were not yet fully known.

INCREASING RESPONSIBILITY

Ethical considerations tend to lag behind scientific advances. According to ethicist Kenneth Vaux, our technological potentials "are frightening for one simple reason: they enlarge our responsibility."[7] Ethicist Joseph Fletcher elaborates on this point: "As medicine's achievements proliferate, and as its control of life, health, and death increases, the frequency, complexity, and subtlety of its decision making also necessarily increase."[8]

Medical ethics have been discussed since ancient times. In the fourth century B.C., the Greek physician Hippocrates developed his Hippocratic oath to guide physicians in their dealings with patients. The oath has survived to the present day, and one of its major tenets, "Do no harm," is still quoted widely.

Through the years, other individuals and groups of professionals devoted to health care developed codes and standards of practice based on ethics. The American Hospital Association (AHA) produced a Patient's Bill of Rights in 1972. This bill stressed the need to inform patients clearly about their condition and treatment options so they can be actively involved in making decisions. A patients' bill of rights has been devised for the elderly in nursing homes. Special ethical codes also guide people involved in genetics, reproductive technology, and organ transplantation as well as researchers who work with human subjects.

Developments in the late twentieth century have increased concern about bioethical issues, by individuals and by groups— "think tanks," policy foundations, and ethics departments within corporations. The government has formed both permanent and temporary groups to examine and formulate bioethical policies.

As more technology becomes available, ethicists are asking

whether a certain device or procedure should be used just because it exists. Should any restraints be put on the kinds of technologies we develop? Are some types of research (for example, cloning) so menacing they should never be explored?

Each area of health care and medicine engenders its own questions. Difficult issues surround genetic technology, as critics challenge the idea that humans have a right to alter life-forms or try to create new ones. They worry about unforeseen, negative consequences if we eliminate certain genes or organisms forever or cross boundaries between the genes of different species.

Then there are the new reproductive technologies and practices, the right of patients to consent to or refuse treatment, and the use of life-sustaining technology. Issues regarding individual patients can be especially complex, since each situation is different, and there may be many choices.

Some issues concern the health care system as a whole: What is the proper role of medical care—to cure specific diseases or to deal with any condition that hinders a person's comfort and happiness? People debate whether there should be any limit to the rights people have in regard to health care—for example, is there a right to have a child, even if a person is infertile or incapable of caring for a child after its birth? Some ethicists think individual interests dominate America's health care system and that we should allocate resources in ways that promote the well-being of society as a whole.

WHO WILL DECIDE?

At the heart of bioethical issues is a fundamental question: Who decides? Bioethicists point out that ethical decisions will be made and health care priorities will be set. That process can either be done through consensus, after open debate, or on a haphazard basis. Decisions about science can be made by the larger society or by military and political leaders, corporations that have power and money, health insurance companies. Their interests may conflict with those of individuals or society in general.

The decisions we make may greatly affect our personal well-being, careers, families, finances, and the health care system as a whole. Bioethical issues affect us all, not just patients and health care professionals. As family members, taxpayers, voters, and citizens, we have a stake in these matters.

Many bioethical dilemmas have no easy answers. People struggle as they make decisions. The implications may be enormous, as when deciding whether to extend the life of a very ill newborn or choosing who shall receive an organ for transplant. Nonetheless, these issues must be faced, especially as technology gives us more and more control over our destiny.

T W O
Reshaping Genetics

PROBABLY NO FIELD OFFERS MORE PROMISE FOR IM-
proving the quality of life, while raising more ethical concerns,
than genetics. Through genetic manipulation—the process of
changing the molecular functioning of organisms—scientists can
control life in ways that were once the domain of science fiction.
Genetic screening has allowed babies to be born healthier, while genetically engineered drugs have extended numerous lives. Scientists
expect to find new ways to prevent and cure devastating diseases.

Here are some ways in which genetics can affect our lives:

*In 1994, a genetically engineered substance called bovine
growth hormone (BGH) was approved for use in dairy cows and
has been used to increase milk production. Many consumers dislike
the idea of using milk that comes from cows who have received the
hormone. Some representatives of milk companies have opposed
the idea of labelling foods to show whether or not the cows received BGH. Should such foods be labelled or not?*

Scientists are working to develop new treatments for genetic diseases. Some diseases are quite rare, affecting hundreds or a few thousand people at most. Is it ethical to spend millions of dollars on research that may benefit only a small segment of the population? Should priorities be set? Who should decide and how?

MILESTONES IN GENETIC RESEARCH

For centuries, people had wondered how traits were passed on from parents to offspring. They did not know what part of the body contained this vital information or how it was transmitted.

In the mid-1800s, clues began to emerge. An Austrian monk named Gregor Mendel studied heredity systematically. For years, he grew pea plants and recorded the traits—colors, shapes of peas, sizes of plants—in each generation. Mendel recognized patterns that he called "laws of inheritance." He noted that some traits disappeared in one generation, then reappeared in later ones. Other traits passed on, unchanged. In 1865, Mendel described his studies in a landmark scientific paper.

During the 1880s, Dutch botanist and geneticist Hugo de Vries investigated heredity to find out why new generations of plants sometimes developed traits that differed from normal ones. De Vries called such changes mutations, from the Latin word *mutare*. He theorized that different traits must be located on some part of the plant in such a way that they could be passed on in separate units.

Eventually, scientists would identify these hereditary units and call them genes. They would learn that genes made up chromosomes, the long, coiled, threadlike structures found in living cells and in viruses. In 1902, Walter S. Sutton announced that chromosomes came in pairs. Human cells contain 46 chromosomes, more accurately viewed as 23 pairs. A normal human egg cell and human sperm contain 23 chromosomes each, forming a total of 46 when they unite during fertilization.

Further research in the early 1900s by the Nobel-prize-winning geneticist Thomas Hunt Morgan and his group of researchers showed that traits were not always passed on as separate units. Some were linked and were passed on together. Using millions of fruit flies, Morgan and his associates studied linkage and mutations, such as crooked bodies and unusually small wings. They identified where traits were located on the fly chromosomes, thus developing the first gene maps. Two decades later, in 1927, Morgan's colleague Herman Muller went on to show how X rays could cause mutations in genes.

By then, scientists had found a substance inside the cell nucleus that seemed to make up chromosomes. They named it DNA, short for deoxyribonucleic acid. Researchers eagerly sought to explain the chemical composition and physical structure of DNA. In 1953, American biologist James Watson and British biophysicist Francis Crick developed a three-dimensional model of the DNA molecule and a theory to explain how it transmitted genetic traits. Critical to their discovery were X-ray diffraction photographs of crystallized DNA taken at King's College in London by Rosalind Franklin and Maurice Wilkins.

The Watson-Crick model revolutionized the field of molecular biology. Within decades, scientists learned a great deal about how DNA guides the manufacturing of cell proteins, used in hormones and enzymes, and how errors in this process can cause disease and disability. Knowing how DNA coded instructions to the cell opened up the field of genetic engineering. Genes were like blueprints for protein synthesis. By manipulating the genes, scientists could change the kind of instructions the DNA "gives" to a cell.

In 1971, biochemist Paul Berg constructed the first recombinant DNA molecule. He took parts of DNA from different species, then put them together with a technique called gene splicing. Using recombinant DNA techniques, scientists have learned how to move genes to new positions along chromosomes. During the process, they can view chromosomes with high-powered electronic microscopes but rely on chemical tracers to locate the DNA itself.

Amazing things have been done. In 1983, scientists produced a "supermouse"—about twice the normal size—by inserting a human growth-cell gene into mice embryos. This was the first time a human gene had functioned in another animal. In 1995, by manipulating fruit fly genes, scientists produced flies that had complete eyes on their wings, legs, and even the tips of their antennae.

From the start, scientists hoped that genetic research would enable them to discover the causes of genetic diseases and even find some way to replace sick genes with healthy ones. They looked forward to finding new cures for diseases, perhaps by permanently altering defective genes. As different genes have been identified, scientists have used the intricate processes of genetic engineering and gene therapy to treat health problems.

GENETIC ENGINEERING

Using genetic engineering, scientists can create large quantities of enzymes and hormones in a laboratory. These are substances that would be produced in a healthy person's body but in small amounts. The technique involves extracting DNA from white blood cells and cutting it with restriction enzymes—substances that trigger or speed up chemical processes. These special enzymes act as molecular "scissors" so that the gene of interest—for example, the gene that directs production of interferon, an antiviral substance—is isolated. Then a bacterial cell is cut in a similar way so that the gene can be "spliced" into the bacterial cell where it will be replicated. When enough of the gene has been produced, it is extracted from the bacterial cell.

In 1978, scientists at Genentech, Inc., a genetic engineering firm in California, succeeded in making insulin from recombinant DNA. The hormone insulin is normally produced by the pancreas and stimulates cells to absorb glucose, a sugar, in the blood. More than eleven million people suffer from diabetes worldwide. They once relied on insulin made from animal products, but many are allergic to it and the supply was sometimes inadequate.

Scientists anticipate using recombinant DNA to help people with depressed immune systems—for example, patients receiving chemotherapy for cancer. The scientists are seeking substances that would protect healthy cells while allowing cancer cells to be destroyed with interferon and powerful anticancer drugs.

Using drugs to treat well-defined illnesses has not stirred much controversy, but some genetically engineered materials do raise concerns. During the 1990s, people worried about the potential misuse of synthetic human growth hormone. Genentech, Inc. developed a form of growth hormone called Protropin, which was approved by the Food and Drug Administration for use in treating dwarfism, an inherited condition in which the pituitary gland does not produce enough growth hormone. Protropin has also been used to help children who suffer from chronic renal insufficiency, a condition that depresses growth.

In 1992, Genentech and its distributor, Caremark, Inc., began sponsoring height screenings in public schools. The shortest students were sent to doctors for evaluations. By 1994, some 20,000 American children had taken growth hormone, which costs about $30,000 per person per year.

Critics complained that Protropin had been given to children who were merely short in stature, not lacking in hormones. The drug has also been used by body builders and athletes. Medical ethics expert Eric Juengst of the University of California at San Francisco said, "The problem is: Who gets it? Those with pituitary dwarfism? How about using it on kids who are marginally short?"[1]

At a congressional hearing held on this matter, legislators raised legal, ethical, and scientific questions. They criticized the promotion of the drug and asked whether people had been misled about its purpose. Representative Ron Wyden (D-Oregon) said, "This is a growing kind of practice that needs some standards."[2] Eric Juengst and others also say that clear guidelines need to be set regarding the use of controversial new products, especially when high profits are at stake.

GENETICALLY ENGINEERED FOODS

Humans have been "engineering" plants for centuries, through techniques such as selective breeding and cloning. However, sophisticated new technology allows scientists to change the genetic code of plants by inserting genes from other plants or even animals. Genetic engineering could produce stronger and more nutritious crops, for instance corn that resists blight or wheat and rice with a higher protein content. Since more than six billion people now inhabit the earth, an adequate food supply is important.

The most heated bioethical debates surround changing the genes of plants and animals that are used for food—for instance, giving cows bovine growth hormone to induce higher milk production. Genetically engineered tomatoes have also come under fire, since scientists found a way to deactivate a gene that causes the fruit to soften and rot. These tomatoes last weeks longer than other tomatoes, and some people prefer their taste as well.

The Pure Food Campaign, a Washington, D.C., consumer group, has opposed all genetically engineered food. They suggest that at the very least, products must be labelled so that consumers can make informed decisions. But producers of some genetically engineered tomatoes object, pointing out that their product contains no foreign genes; they have merely "turned off" the ripening gene already in the tomato.[3] Other foods do contain altered genes.

Critics say that nobody can predict all the future effects, whether positive or negative, of changing plant or animal genes. Therefore, some scientists say we should focus on population control and ways to better use and distribute the world's food supply.

New concerns were raised late in 1995 when the U.S. Agriculture Department moved to make it easier for researchers to field test genetically engineered plants. Old rules had required scientists to seek special permits for such tests, during which they study how new plants perform. Receiving a permit often took several months. Under new rules, researchers need only give the department notice of any planned tests. The department would have thirty days to object. Instead of filing reports on every test, they would need to report only unusual results. The Environmental Defense Fund was among the groups that said these new rules could reduce public awareness of biotechnological research and would increase the chances of disrupting the ecological balance.

GENE THERAPY

Therapeutic uses of DNA research focus on ways to treat diseases. There are two main types of gene therapy, which basically involves inserting a specific gene into a cell in order to repair a problem and restore function. Somatic cell therapy involves using a bit of genetic material to cure a patient of a particular disease. Germ cell therapy, a more controversial process, deals with the source of the condition by getting rid of a gene in the patient's egg or sperm cell so the defect cannot be passed on to new generations.

Scientists have used gene therapy on Lesch-Nyhan syndrome, a rare disease that causes mental retardation, palsy, and self-mutilating behavior. It results from a defect in a gene that produces an enzyme needed to digest protein. Without this enzyme, substances called purines build up and destroy nerve tissue. In 1983, some researchers in California inserted a healthy gene into a batch of defective cells from a Lesch-Nyhan patient. They had first used a gene-splicing technique to put a healthy gene for the enzyme into a mouse leukemia virus, after modifying that virus so it would not cause cancer. The cells began to manufacture the missing enzyme, as researchers had predicted.

During the 1990s, scientists used experimental gene therapy to treat a devastating immune system disorder in which infants are born without the gene to make the necessary enzyme adenosine deaminase (ADA). Scientists took cells from an infant's placenta shortly after birth, then inserted an ADA gene into the cells. The cells were then transfused into the baby. A year after treatment, a girl who received treatment had a functioning immune system, although she needed to have regular transfusions of white blood cells to remain healthy.

By 1993, scientists had succeeded in halting muscle deterioration in mice by inserting a nondefective gene, something that might fight two forms of muscular dystrophy. Scientists now know the gene for muscular dystrophy, which protein is coded by that gene, and how the protein is constructed.

Viruses are often used to deliver new genes into a cell because they contain the machinery needed to infect a cell gene. Yet viruses are not often selective about which cells they infect. In 1994, scientist Yuet Wai Kan of the University of California at San Francisco found a virus that, in a test tube, was selective enough to be used to target particular human blood cells.

Genetic engineering seems boundless. As scientists identify and locate genes, they can remove and replace specific chromosomal material in human cells. Genetically engineered vaccines might prevent malaria, hepatitis, amoebic dysentery, and AIDS. Gene splicing may cure sickle-cell anemia, using one new gene to correct the defect in the red blood cell and another to build the body's resistance to a drug that would kill defective genes. Therapies for AIDS and other major diseases could relieve enormous suffering.

GERM CELL MANIPULATION

Most gene therapy deals with cells like those in the lung or liver, which will die with a person. Manipulation of germ cells—eggs and sperm that pass on hereditary traits—stirs far more debate. In 1994, scientists at the University of Pennsylvania manipulated stem cells—early-stage sperm cells that reside in the testes and are the source of all sperm produced by males. When genes in these cells are changed, those changes are passed on to any offspring, in effect changing the organism's genetic inheritance.

These scientists, who have applied for a government patent, altered the genes in mice sperm cells in order to study the process of sperm development. They hope such research will lead to better treatments for infertility and genetic disorders in humans. The process might also prove useful for commercial breeding of animals.

Opponents of such research oppose techniques that alter a person's basic genetic nature. They believe altering egg or sperm cells could unleash a genetic mistake on future generations, making it far too risky. They also fear pressure on scientists to use such techniques to "enhance" human beings. Genes may have other purposes we do not fully understand, and the deliberate extinction of a gene might have unforeseen, negative consequences.

Critics also offer religious objections, saying that such activities oppose God's will. In 1980, Pope John Paul II said that modifying genes is "against the well-being of humanity. This is shown in the domain of genetic manipulations and biological experimentation as well as in the research of chemical, bacteriological and nuclear warfare." He condemned "any act which leads to the suppression of the newborn disabled person" as "a breach not only of medical ethics but also of the fundamental and inalienable right to life."[4]

Others express similar misgivings. The National Council of Churches' Task Force on Human Life and the New Genetics said that new genetic engineering methods "challenge our understanding of the nature of personal identity, the meaning of human community, the inviolability of the body, the structure of human parenthood, and the limits on human intervention into natural processes."[5]

Supporters claim that gene therapy is no different from or worse than other medical treatments. They believe people have the right to use technology that can help them or their future offspring. There may be economic benefits if modifying germ cells costs less than using gene therapy on a person later, after a disease has developed. Besides, say supporters, scientific knowledge is valuable for its own sake and should be allowed in a free society. In response to fears about possible risks of germ-line therapy on the human gene pool, supporters respond that some genetic diseases are so horrible that new genetic techniques are well justified.

CONCERNS ABOUT CLONING

In 1961, a British scientist manipulated frog eggs to produce two identical tadpoles—clones of each other. Twenty years later, Nobel laureate James D. Watson, co-discoverer of the structure of DNA, said, "A human being—born of clonal reproduction—most likely will appear on earth within twenty to fifty years."[6] Watson expressed concern about this possibility and called for international research guidelines on cloning. The National Institutes of Health did devise guidelines for cloning in laboratory work.

Perhaps the most familiar examples of clones can be seen in many of the plants for sale at local stores. Plant tissues are often cultured to produce clones of various plants. Creating identical organisms, whether plant or animal, involves the restructuring of an egg. Scientists remove the nucleus and replace it with the cell of the organism to be cloned. The cell holds a set of genes and must be transplanted so as not to damage the egg. The egg is activated so an embryo results. In animals, the embryo is then placed inside a uterus to develop. Identical twins are naturally occurring clones, but there are many people who want to ban any research relating to the intentional cloning of human beings.

In a highly publicized 1993 experiment, scientists at George Washington University Medical Center in Washington, D.C., made clones by splitting a human embryo that contained both male and female cells. They cloned embryos by first splitting seventeen chromosomally abnormal early-stage embryos, consisting of a few cells, into forty-eight single cells, called blastomeres. Using an artificial gel coating, the team was able to coax a few cells to continue to divide, reaching the thirty-two-cell stage.

After six days, all had died. Yet, for the first time, human embryos had been cloned. Scientists had been able to remove the protective coating of the human egg and replace it with an artificial one. The cells might have continued to grow had they been normal and been placed in a human uterus. Such methods might enable doctors to create twins and other multiples and improve the chances of a successful pregnancy through in vitro fertilization. Some people support cloning as a way to produce more organs for transplants or to specially design people to fit certain roles.

Dr. Jerry Hall, director of the experiment, acknowledged that it had troubled many people, but said, "I think the positive side is that it had made people more aware of the basics of embryology and of the methods used in in vitro fertilization."[7]

Opponents of cloning argue each human is meant to be unique, with an individual identity. Cloned people might feel upset about their genetic origins. Cloning with eggs alone might result in an imbalance of females and affect attitudes about the roles of males and females in reproduction. It might allow us to determine in advance what kind of people and world we should have. A market for cloned embryos might develop, and it would be possible to give birth to twins or triplets separately, years apart. Imagine the psychological problems that could arise from such situations.

John A. Robertson, professor of law at the University of Texas, Austin, points out that the billion-dollar infertility industry is largely unregulated and "scientific zeal and the profit motive combine with the desire of infertile couples for biologic offspring to create an enormous power to manipulate the earliest stages of human life."[8] Yet Robertson considers some cloning research acceptable if we carefully examine how it will be used. Other supporters point out that if we understand what is involved with cloning, we can pass laws to prevent negative consequences, just as we can pass laws regulating other biomedical matters.

PATENTING NEW LIFE-FORMS

Now that scientists can genetically engineer new life-forms, should people be able to patent them? The patent law of 1793, revised in 1952, protects the "new and useful manufacture of composition of matter." But people question whether it should apply to living things, such as microorganisms, as well as tools or machines.

Companies spend large sums of money on genetic research and hope to develop valuable commercial properties. In the 1970s, scientists at General Electric Company produced an oil-eating bacteria from research with microorganisms. In 1979, microbiologist Dr. Ananda M. Chakrabarty applied for a patent for the bacteria.

The U.S. Patent and Trademark Office declined to grant the patent on the basis that there are so many living things that vast numbers could become the objects of patent applications. The Court of Customs and Patent Appeals overruled the government, and the case reached the Supreme Court in 1980. In a five to four decision, the Court ruled that forms of life created in a laboratory may indeed be patented. The Court stressed the importance of encouraging scientific research and development that will aid humankind.

The Court specifically said that scientific ideas, formulas, and theories are not patentable, nor are physical phenomena and the laws of nature. The difference, said the Court, was that oil-eating bacteria were "non-naturally occurring" but were rather a "product of human ingenuity having a distinctive name, character, and use."[9]

Similar patents have been issued since this 1980 decision. Companies such as Genentech, Inc., applauded the Court's verdict, which enabled them to patent certain gene-splicing procedures that led to the development of interferon, insulin, and human growth hormone. Dr. Chakrabarty went on to new genetic research aimed at finding microorganisms that might rid soil and water of toxic chemical residues. As interest in genetic research has increased, shares in such companies has earned millions for some early investors.

A slightly different question arises as to the ownership of new life-forms when scientists use cells they have obtained from human donation. Debates on these matters are likely to continue.

LINGERING QUESTIONS

People have tried to weigh the risks and benefits of genetic research and technology. Might the treatments cause, as well as alleviate, problems? Is there some kind of genetic research that should never be done, such as stem-cell manipulation or human cloning? What precautions should we take and what guidelines should we set? Who should set the guidelines or monitor research?

The results of creating new life-forms may be unpredictable. Consider a bacteria that promises to manage oil spills by digesting oil and turning it into a form other marine life will eat. After the oil is gone, the bacteria supposedly will die, but nobody is sure what else might happen. New and unproven microorganisms could behave differently outside the laboratory, leading to pollution or disease. There is no sure way to know or to control such things.

Many people think the perils of genetic technology have been overstated and, often, ungrounded. Says Celine Gelinas, a molecular biologist in New Jersey, "If you look at the beginning of recombinant DNA technology, there was this big fear that this was going to be terrible. And it turned out that it brought a lot more good than any problems."[10]

Other scientists note that decisions are not made arbitrarily. Research centers have institutional review boards that often include members of the community. They analyze research proposals and must approve them before scientists can go forward.

Bioethicists point out that certain groups of people may be shut out of genetic treatments. Jonathan Moreno, an ethicist at the Hastings Center, a bioethical think tank, says, "Access to the elimination of genetic disease will be quite expensive for a long time. [Low-income people] won't have access."[11]

■   ■   ■

Clearly, genetic technology has profound implications. Decisions in this area could have dramatic and unpredictable effects on the human gene pool and many other areas of life.

How do nonscientists feel about genetic issues? In a 1992 poll conducted by the March of Dimes, an organization that works to prevent birth defects and help people to deal with them, more than 40 percent of all Americans favored using gene therapy to improve the physical and intellectual characteristics of their children. According to author Richard Liebmann-Smith, "What makes this especially scary is that when it comes to modern genetics, the American people—by their own admission—simply haven't got a clue. Despite their eagerness to embrace gene therapy to beef up the looks and I.Q.s of their kids, an alarming 86 percent of those polled confessed to knowing 'relatively little' or 'almost nothing' about it."[12]

Questions about genetic engineering and research are not likely to go away, nor will ignorance about these and other bioethical matters serve us well. As authors David Suzuki and Peter Knudtson say, "Everyone must share responsibility for the decisions that will increasingly shape the genetic future of our planet."[13]

THREE
To Know or Not to Know

While conducting tests on a husband and wife to discover why their child has a genetic disease, doctors realize that the husband could not be the child's biological father. Should they inform the wife, husband, both, or neither?

■

A couple, both dwarfs, seek genetic testing during the wife's pregnancy. They want a child who is also a dwarf, with one normal gene and one mutant gene for dwarfism. They plan to abort a fetus that has either two nondwarf genes or two mutant genes, a condition that usually causes death during infancy. Should the test be done under these circumstances? What about the abortion?

Imagine a world in which we all can obtain a computerized printout that spells out our genetic code and predicts our future health. Or we may get a precise genetic profile of an unborn child, perhaps within days of conception. Such information may be available in the near future, as scientists continue to identify various genes and discover their functions.

GENETIC MAPPING

Under the National Institutes of Health, the Human Genome Project was set up in 1988 to locate and identify the genes in a human being, a massive undertaking, since the human genome contains an estimated 80,000 genes. A genome is the sum of all genetic information in a living species, varying from simple (a virus) to very complex (a human being). Scientists from around the world are pooling their talents to map the genes—figure out the sequences of the three billion pairs of chemical bases.

The U.S. government will spend an estimated $3 billion on the genome project over fifteen years. Critics say that when the government promotes "big science" in this way, smaller research facilities may have trouble competing for funds. Supporters of the genome project say it will provide invaluable information about human growth, development, and aging, as well as lead to new ways of treating disease and improving brain functioning, among other things. Its total cost is just slightly more than the United States spends *each day* on health care.

As they work on the genome, scientists are also identifying abnormal genes. They extract DNA from a sampling of white blood cells, then use restriction enzymes to cut the DNA. The fragments are placed in an electrophoresis gel. When electricity is added to the gel, the fragments of DNA separate. By comparing the patterns of DNA fragments of an affected person's DNA with normal DNA samples, scientists can spot genetic abnormalities that signal disease.

It is estimated that the average person has between five and ten genetic defects, varying from trivial to serious. There are about four thousand genetic diseases, some involving crippling physical or mental conditions that impair a person throughout life. When one or more genes are defective, cells may not receive the instructions to make proteins or enzymes needed for normal growth and development. Minor errors, such as color blindness or birthmarks, occur in 6 to 14 percent of all live births. Forty percent of infant deaths occur because of genetic factors. About 33 percent of all miscarriages occur because of gross chromosomal defects.

SCREENING TESTS

As scientists have identified various genes and their traits, they have devised screening tests for genetic defects. It usually takes about one year after finding a gene to develop a screening test to determine if people carry genes that might lead to certain conditions or be passed on to their children. Tests can also be done prenatally—on an unborn child in the uterus.

By 1995, more than nine hundred genes for inherited diseases had been found. There were tests to detect genes for Fragile X syndrome (a type of mental retardation), Alzheimer's, Huntington's, certain types of heart disease, and several cancers. Blood tests could be done to reveal mutated genes that placed people at high risk for cancer of the breast, colon, thyroid, and ovaries. Another test showed an inherited tendency to get brain tumors.

By the year 2010, there may be tests for hundreds of conditions, including a type of high blood pressure, rheumatoid arthritis, dyslexia (a learning disability), and schizophrenia (a mental illness). A complete genetic map may be available by the year 2030 or 2040. Such a map would show us, at birth, what diseases we are sure to get or not get, the likelihood of getting certain other diseases—and perhaps the condition that may later cause our death.

In 1995, OncorMed, a biotechnology company in Maryland, devised computer programs that can identify people whose family histories show they are at high risk of cancer. Those people could then be tested for cancer-causing genes. Dr. Timothy Triche, chief executive officer of OncorMed, said that individuals with the gene could be screened more often and at earlier ages.[1] Advocates of such testing say it will enable those people at risk to take positive actions to delay or prevent illnesses. Counselors would answer questions and help patients deal with the emotional aspects of the testing.

For others, the matter is less clear-cut. For instance, it has long been known that some types of breast cancer run in families. Having a close relative, a mother or sister, with breast cancer greatly increases the risk. Hereditary breast cancers may occur at relatively young ages and progress rapidly. There are successful treatments but no cure; doctors can only advise frequent checkups.

By 1994, the breast cancer gene had been identified. Some women at high risk undergo the genetic screening test, while others do not want to know. Certainly, psychological trauma can result from positive test results—in some cases, women attempted suicide after learning that they had the gene.[2] Other women, after seeing relatives die of breast cancer, choose to have their breasts removed surgically before disease can occur. One who made that choice said that she felt "relieved . . . I took control over my destiny."[3]

In a family at risk for Huntington's disease, one sister took the test; the other did not. Another young adult who decided not to take the test said she would prefer to have a 50-50 chance than to know for sure that she had it: "If I was told that I'm going to get HD when I'm thirty, do you know what every day would be like? Every day would not be a real life. I just couldn't live like that."[4]

Others disagree, saying that this knowledge would help them plan their lives. Those who chose not to marry or have children because of their risk would not have to give up those things if they took a test and it was negative. "Being trapped in limbo makes me have sort of a half-life," said a woman in her thirties.[5]

Some experts believe genetic screening tests should not be used until ethical issues are resolved. Dr. Francis Collins of the National Institutes of Health and director of the Human Genome Project says, "The professional genetics community, the Human Genome Council, and the National Breast Council Coalition have stated that these tests should not now be made available."[6]

Other experts say testing should be done only in research settings where patients can consult with counselors before and after the tests. Dr. Gail Vance, a biochemist at the Indiana University School of Medicine, said, "As has happened in the past with genetics, the technology far precedes the response to what we're going to do with the technology."[7]

Supporters of genetic testing say it is unethical to refuse testing if it is available and people want it. Dr. David Sidransky, a cancer researcher at Johns Hopkins University, said, "Information is neutral. We always have this question: Is it good or bad? We don't know until we use it. . . . The medical risks are zero."[8]

CONCERN ABOUT THE USES OF SCREENING INFORMATION

More precise genetic tests mean more precise information, potentially from before birth onward. Personal information may come into the wrong hands, raising privacy issues, and genetic information could be used to discriminate against people in various ways.

For example, during the 1970s, the U.S. Air Force Academy and some airlines refused to accept applicants who had the genetic trait for sickle-cell anemia. They reasoned that people with this defect in their red blood cells, which carry oxygen, would suffer from oxygen deprivation at high altitudes. However, no conclusive scientific research supported this contention.

In 1990, Theresa Morelli applied for health insurance and was turned down. The company said she could not receive coverage because her father had been diagnosed with Huntington's disease. They would only insure Morelli if she reached age fifty without showing signs of Huntington's. Morelli, an attorney, worked to change the law in her state, Ohio.[9]

Addressing the potential uses of genetic information, Kenneth Offit, chief of the clinical genetics service at Memorial Sloan-

Kettering Cancer Center, says that the same information that could help people to prevent possible genetic diseases could, if given to an insurance company, "mean the loss of medical coverage since it would constitute evidence of a pre-existing condition."[10] In a 1993 survey, insurance companies in thirty-two states said that a family history of breast cancer was an acceptable reason to deny coverage.[11] In 1992, Montana outlawed such discrimination; Ohio banned it the next year. Wisconsin, Oregon, and California have strong genetic privacy acts that ban the release of any genetic information without a patient's written permission. Insurance companies may not refuse a person based on information from genetic testing. Other states are considering such laws, and Congress has debated passing national genetic privacy legislation.

What if testing is done without a person's knowledge? Tests are becoming increasingly sophisticated. Some can be done with a small amount of blood, a hair, or a tissue sample. The FBI and the U.S. Army have DNA databanks. In some states, ex-convicts give DNA samples as a condition of parole. People also give blood samples during routine physicals and when applying for life insurance.

There are disadvantages in knowing all our possible disease genes and susceptibilities. George Annas, director of Boston University's law, medicine, and ethics program, says that the ability to know our future could change our self-concept as well as the way that others view us.[12]

Because people might be stigmatized and discriminated against on the basis of their genes, Annas thinks the federal government should create an agency to develop genetic privacy guidelines. The growth of new communication arenas using computers raises even more privacy issues. Noting the potential for commercial abuse of genetic testing, Offit recommends that medical professionals, federal agencies, and consumers unite to set standards and plan ways to combine genetic testing with proper counseling.[13]

A related privacy issue involves who should have access to DNA fingerprints. The American public heard a great deal about

DNA fingerprinting during the 1994–1995 trial of O. J. Simpson, who was accused of murdering his ex-wife Nicole Brown and her friend Ronald Goldman. The prosecution presented evidence that DNA found in blood at the murder scene was consistent with Simpson's and that DNA from bloodstains found in Simpson's car could be a match for that of Simpson and one of the victims. DNA testing has become a routine part of the criminal justice system and has been used in many cases to acquit people accused of crimes, as well as to convict them. In the Simpson case, where a jury reached a "not guilty" verdict, defense attorneys had argued that DNA evidence was unreliable because of possible police misconduct and sloppy laboratory procedures.

GENETIC SCREENING AND EMPLOYMENT

Should genetic testing be required as part of a job application? Some companies say that screening could be used to protect people from jobs that might endanger their health. Opponents worry that tests will be used to discriminate against people, not only in jobs but in other ways, such as applications to borrow money for a car or mortgage. Employers might use test results to dismiss employees or deny jobs to certain people. Health risks might keep people out of certain careers, although they might never get the disease.

In 1995, the federal Equal Employment Opportunity Commission (EEOC) said that workers cannot be discriminated against on the basis of their genetic makeup. The EEOC said that using genetic test results to deny employment to people who remain healthy but have a genetic predisposition to a certain disease is illegal under the 1990 Americans With Disabilities Act (ADA). The EEOC manual describes disability laws and defines "disability" and "impairment" in terms of the ADA so that employees, investigators, and others can interpret the law. Having a predisposition to disease is not in itself a disability, says the EEOC, but it can be viewed as one if used to discriminate against a person in regard to employment.

In the wake of the EEOC's statement, Dr. Francis S. Collin, director of the Federal Center for Human Genome Research, said, "I am delighted about this development. Now we can say confidently that this sensitive information cannot be used against people and they don't have to fear genetic testing."[14] Yet questions remain. Having access to screening information could influence employers' minds about whom to hire, even though they might give other reasons for their hiring decisions.

PRENATAL SCREENING

The most common genetic screenings are prenatal tests to check the health of a fetus. Testing is recommended for pregnant women over age thirty-five, when a woman is more prone to have a baby with a genetic problem.

In a procedure called amniocentesis, a needle is used to extract a small amount of fluid from the amniotic sac, which surrounds the developing fetus inside the mother's uterus. Another prenatal test, chorionic villae sampling (CVS), can be performed after about six weeks of pregnancy. Doctors remove a sample of cells from the amniotic fluid by way of the vagina. The fluid can be tested for chromosomal abnormalities and certain diseases, such as sickle-cell anemia (an abnormality on the gene controlling the shape of red blood cells). New blood tests and other techniques are being devised to give more accurate genetic information at even earlier stages of pregnancy.

More than three thousand genetic diseases lead to retardation or crippling physical conditions. Five percent of all live births involve these kinds of problems. A couple has about a 3 percent risk of having a genetically defective child.

The wrong number of chromosomes can impair growth and development. An extra chromosome number 21 results in Down Syndrome, which can involve various physical and mental disabilities. An extra number 13 leads to mental retardation, a small, deformed head, and an extra finger on each hand. Infants with too few chromosomes often die before, or soon after, birth.

Tay-Sachs disease can also be diagnosed in the uterus. This devastating disease strikes at about six months of age, causing retardation, paralysis, blindness, deafness, convulsions, then death, usually by age four. Fatty material builds up in the central nervous system because an enzyme that normally breaks down these fats is not produced. A child must inherit a Tay-Sachs gene from both parents in order to get the disease, which is most common among eastern and central European Jews. One in every 3,600 Jewish pregnancies is affected by Tay-Sachs, with one in every 360,000 among non-Jews.

SCREENING EMBRYOS

Scientists can now test embryos—fertilized eggs made up of only a few cells—for genetic disorders. To do so, they fertilize eggs in vitro, then allow them to grow to the eight-cell stage, at which time they are still small enough to fit on a pinhead. They remove one or two cells and analyze the chromosomes by copying the gene in question or by injecting fluorescent DNA probes that can be made to home in on certain mutations. Acceptable embryos are then implanted into a woman, usually more than one at a time. The process has been completed in just one day. New tests may require only thirty minutes.

A dilemma emerges if people begin to screen embryos when no special risk is involved, perhaps to select a boy or girl, or to seek traits fitting their fantasy of an "ideal child." As people limit their families to one or two children, they may want a child that fits their desires. On the other hand, women already can have legal abortions during the early months of pregnancy for almost any reason. Embryonic testing allows a woman to end a pregnancy that has just begun, avoiding the decision of a later abortion.

CHOICES AFTER PRENATAL SCREENING

Parents may face difficult choices when test results show serious defects. In some cases, parents refuse prenatal tests because they firmly oppose abortion. To them, the makeup of a fetus should not determine whether or not it is to be born. Some people who oppose abortion have screening tests anyway, in order to prepare themselves for the child's future condition. Others find it acceptable to end a pregnancy when tests show serious defects.

Those who believe that abortion is never justified include leaders of the Roman Catholic Church, certain other religious groups, and individuals who believe that life begins at conception. They view abortion as the taking of a human life. Explaining this position, William Daniel said, "The embryo has life; it is a human embryo, and therefore the life it has is human—not that of some other species. . . . Certainly the embryo is only a potential baby, just as a baby is only a potential adult. . . . the biological continuity between all three [embryo, baby, adult] is total and unbroken."[15]

Other people accept abortion in certain circumstances—rape, incest, health risks to the mother, a serious health problem of the fetus. Still others think abortion should be available at a woman's request. Abortion supporters say that the rights of the mother not to continue a pregnancy outweigh the rights of a fetus not yet born.

In *Roe v. Wade*, on January 22, 1973, the Supreme Court ruled that states may not ban abortion during the first trimester, or three months, of pregnancy. Some regulation is possible during the next trimester when a fetus may be capable of living outside the uterus. States may forbid abortion after the first six months but are not required to do so. Antiabortionists have renewed the debate over the age of viability—the time at which a fetus can survive outside the uterus. New technology has made it possible for fetuses to survive outside the uterus at increasingly earlier ages.

When does life begin? Some say at fertilization, when the sperm and egg unite, since all the genetic information needed for a new and unique being is present. Organ systems begin developing. Within weeks, the heart is beating; at about ten weeks, the fetus moves; by twelve weeks it can swallow, urinate, and suck its thumb. Others say life begins at birth. Some say it occurs when a soul develops, and different religions disagree about when that occurs. Some scientists say life begins when the brain starts to function and note that brain-wave activity has been detected by the twelfth week of pregnancy.

In 1981, members of a congressional subcommittee sought a constitutional amendment saying that life begins at conception. They received support from scientists and physicians who claimed that, from a biological point of view, life does begin at conception. Other scientists say this question is metaphysical and religious in nature, not scientific. The National Academy of Sciences has said that scientists should not decide this question.

According to bioethicist Thomas Shannon, people differ on the abortion issue depending on "the extent to which . . . [they believe] biological realities can be manipulated, controlled, and set aside. . . . The trend toward abortion on request reflects the most recent tendency in modern thought—namely, the attempt to subordinate biology to reason, to bring it under control, to master it."[16]

Those who find it acceptable to abort fetuses with serious problems say parents and society have a duty to reduce suffering and to prevent genetic defects from plaguing more generations. While some people say a child has the right to begin life with a sound mind and a sound body,[17] others say that humankind has no right to prevent genetic tragedies; misfortunes occur for a reason.

Does society have a stake in preventing certain diseases, whether contagious or genetic? Laws that prevent people with certain genetic conditions from having children would conflict with their right to make their own decisions. Yet society already controls certain areas of health by requiring immunizations, quarantines, hospitalization, detention of people trying to enter the country, and treatment for venereal disease.

Those who want to prevent the births of people with serious genetic defects say that decisions could be made according to the amount of pain and suffering, severity of problems, mortality rates, amount of dependency during one's lifetime, cost, and age of onset of various conditions. Control could be exercised through mandatory genetic screening before marriage, before conception, or after conception; giving parents genetic information and allowing them to choose; imposed sterilization, contraception, and/or abortion. But who should have the right to establish such controls? Mandatory control goes against America's legal and moral traditions, say civil liberties advocates.

The issue is complicated by the fact that genetic tests are not always clear-cut. Abnormal chromosomal patterns may lead to different results in a person, ranging from mild problems to severe. Tests may also be wrong. In some cases, a couple who had received test results showing no abnormalities sued the testing centers after their child was born deformed.

Screening has led to a dramatic decrease in the number of Tay-Sachs babies, only five each year in North America. One couple whose first child died from Tay-Sachs underwent screening tests during the next two pregnancies. They had decided it was immoral to let another child suffer like their firstborn had. "People may judge us for deciding we would abort a fetus that was positive for Tay-Sachs but they don't know the horror we went through. I would never allow a child to suffer like that again knowing there was a way to prevent it," said the thirty-three-year-old mother.

While certain conditions are devastating, disturbing issues arise about the kinds of traits parents might reject. In a 1990 survey conducted by the Shriver Center for Mental Retardation, 12 percent of those polled would abort a fetus if they found that it possessed a gene for an untreatable form of obesity (such a gene has *not* been found). Most physicians find this kind of thinking unethical.[18]

There are fears that humans might try to manipulate reproduction so that only "perfect" children are born. This implies a rejection and lack of compassion toward people who don't reach an arbitrary standard or who have mental and physical handicaps or low IQs. And now there is even talk of judging people by a new standard—the EQ, or emotional quotient. Ethicist Andrew Kimbrell expresses concern, saying, "It's commercial eugenics—the selling of the idea of perfect children, perfect babies, the perfect body to the American public."[19]

Canadian biologist N. J. Berill made this chilling prediction in the 1960s: "Sooner or later one human society or another will launch out on this adventure [of using genetics to produce people with certain traits], whether the rest of mankind approves or not. If this happens, and a superior race emerges with greater intelligence and longer lives, how will these people look upon those who are lagging behind? One thing is certain: they, not we, will be the heirs to the future, and they will assume control."[20]

GENETIC SCREENING AND CHILDREN

In 1994, researchers had to decide whether children should be told they carried a gene that gave them an 85 percent chance of developing breast cancer as adults. A screening test enabled researchers to determine that certain parents and children had this gene. They decided not to tell the families because there is no known way to prevent the cancer. Yet some families were angry when they found out they had not been told. At the heart of this debate is a recurring bioethical question: Who makes the decision?

Dr. Barbara Weber of the University of Pennsylvania School of Medicine said that she and her colleagues had decided to inform only those women over age eighteen who requested their test results. She worried that young people with positive tests would experience fear and a changed outlook on life.[21]

Others have different viewpoints. Mary Z. Pelias, a lawyer and professor of genetics at Louisiana State University, said that *parents* should decide what to tell their children, rather than geneticists or ethicists.[22] Pelias says that constitutional law and family law support her position. Health care personnel can counsel the parents, give them information, and make sure they understand, "but after we have done that, we have done our professional best, and then we should step back," she says.[23]

How might people use genetic testing of children? It is conceivable that adoptive parents might request such screening as part of the health exam that is given during the adoption process, especially if the adoptive child is from a foreign country.

Dr. Dorothy C. Wertz, senior scientist at the Shriver Center for Mental Retardation in Waltham, Massachusetts, is among those who believe genetic testing should not be done on a child unless a clear medical benefit will result. A condition that fits this model is hypercholesterolemia, in which excess cholesterol in the blood can be controlled with treatment and lifestyle changes. Wertz and others oppose testing in cases where scientists can merely predict without offering any help. She warns against the belief that "knowledge is good in itself."[24]

But when Wertz asked parents visiting prenatal testing clinics if they thought parents should have children tested for a disease like Alzheimer's, 61 percent said yes; 47 percent said they would tell children the results. They had been warned that by doing so, the children could suffer emotionally and psychologically. Families that already had such genetic disorders expressed more reluctance to tell their children.

During 1995, the American Society of Human Genetics began work on a position paper dealing with the issue of genetic testing of children. Advocacy groups for people with genetic disorders and families with at least one member so affected were among those asked to contribute their opinions to a panel assembled by the Human Genome Project. This is one of several ethical matters that the project has addressed. About 5 percent of the genome project budget is being used for studies of related bioethical issues.

Then, too, should people who find out they have a genetic condition be required to tell the members of their family? A parent who realizes he or she has an inherited disease and who has adult children may have to decide whether to tell them before they marry and have their own children. Health care professionals also may face the dilemma of whether or not to breach ethics regarding patient confidentiality and inform others who are at risk. As with other bioethical dilemmas, there are no easy answers.

FOUR

Pregnancy at Any Cost?

Mr. and Mrs. B., in their late forties, are newlyweds who want to have a child with their genetic traits. Mrs. B's grown daughter from a previous marriage has offered to donate an egg, which could be fertilized in a lab with Mr. B's sperm, then implanted in a third woman who would act as a surrogate mother and carry the child. What are the pros and cons of such an arrangement?

■

A woman, four months pregnant, has been ignoring medical advice about monitoring her diabetes. Uncontrolled diabetes can harm the fetus, leading to spontaneous abortion, premature birth, or a stillborn infant. Should the doctor seek a court order to force this patient to stay in the hospital for treatment?

■

A couple plans to use prenatal testing to find out the sex of their unborn child. They plan to abort a fetus that is the same sex as their other child. Should doctors perform such a test if they know it is being done for sex-selection? Should they perform an abortion under these circumstances?

Mrs. H., thirteen weeks pregnant, finds out she is going to have triplets, something she and her husband find intolerable. Aware that a procedure called selective termination can eliminate two fetuses, with a small risk that the third will die, she asks that this be done. It involves injecting the unwanted fetuses with a solution that will cause them to die in the uterus. Should the procedure be performed? Would the procedure be more acceptable if the fetuses had serious defects instead of being healthy but unwanted?

Many controversial bioethical issues involve human sexuality and reproduction. People have diverse, deeply held opinions about the extent to which medicine should intervene in reproductive matters.

Knowledge and technology give us more choices about reproduction. Through birth control, we can plan or avoid pregnancy. Abortions end unwanted pregnancies. About 15 percent of all couples who want children are infertile—unable to conceive in the conventional way.

Today, medicine provides ways around this problem—drugs and hormones to stimulate egg or sperm production, surgery to correct blockages. Eggs and sperm can be acquired through donors. Pregnancies can be started in the lab.

On the horizon is reproduction through parthenogenesis—which involves no sperm, just two eggs that are fused and made to divide. This process, a form of reproduction found in some lower animals, would enable a mother to have a female child with her traits only. Two women could have a baby with their combined traits.

Critics wonder how far science should go to help infertile people conceive, what kinds of reproductive technology are acceptable, and who should have access to it—married couples? unmarried couples? single people? Opinions differ.

ARTIFICIAL INSEMINATION

Artificial insemination has been available for decades. Sperm from a husband or other donor can be placed into a woman's reproductive tract during her most fertile days to increase the chances of conception. About 170,000 American women each year use this technique, half using sperm donated by their husbands, the rest using sperm from other donors. Some 65,000 births result.[1]

Ethical issues have arisen, and laws have been passed to define the rights and roles of the parties involved. Who is the actual father of the child? Even when both a husband and wife consent to artificial insemination, some courts regard the child as illegitimate. More than fifteen states have passed laws declaring that the child is legitimate if the husband agreed in writing to the procedure. Laws also bar sperm donors from access to medical records that would show they had fathered a child, nor may they have access to the child. Most donors are anonymous and have no financial responsibility to the children. In divorce cases, courts hold the husband legally responsible for child support.

People have used sperm donation as a way to create offspring with superior intellect or other features. At the Repository for Germinal Choice in California, Robert K. Graham, the inventor of shatter-proof glasses, offered clients sperm from Nobel Prize winners, Olympic medalists, and others with superior endowments. Women using the sperm had to have at least high-average intelligence and the ability to foster achievement in a child. Graham said it was important to provide the world with larger numbers of outstanding individuals. Some of the resulting children have superior intelligence while others do not.

In some cases, sperm donors who "fathered" a child sought visitation rights years after the birth. The donors had given sperm to unmarried female friends who wanted to have a child without becoming sexually involved with a man or going to a sperm bank.

In recent decades, more unmarried women have used sperm

banks. This upsets people with certain religious convictions or beliefs about traditional families. They say children should know who their parents are and that having babies outside of marriage is immoral. They also criticize lesbians who use artificial insemination. Should fertility clinics and sperm banks treat such people differently than they would married men and women? Should it matter whether the clinic is private or receives federal funds?

Some supporters of artificial insemination say that everyone is entitled to receive medical procedures, regardless of whether others approve of their values or lifestyle. They claim that, in a free society, there can be no laws that determine who is a fit parent. But critics might argue that services need not be provided to everybody.

Another concern is that children conceived by the same donor might meet and marry later on, producing children likely to have birth defects because the parents share some of the same genes. This is unlikely, although possible. To prevent this, clinics limit the number of times one donor can contribute sperm. Children who are told how they were conceived can later act on that knowledge, marrying people who know their lineage. But some parents have mixed feelings about telling their children, fearing the emotional impact of realizing one has no identified father.

EGG DONATION

Eggs can also be donated and used by women who cannot produce their own. The donor must take hormones and have frequent medical exams to determine when an egg has ripened and can be removed by aspiration with a needle through the skin.

In 1994, a Scottish scientist announced that he had successfully transplanted ovaries from mice fetuses into adult mice, where they went on to produce eggs that could be fertilized, growing into normal mice. Scientists say we may soon be able to use eggs from the ovaries of aborted fetuses as donor eggs for women. By ten weeks, a female fetus has made all its eggs, a total of six to seven million. After being implanted, an ovary from a fetus would then grow to adult size, although nobody is sure how long that would take or whether it would function exactly as normal.

A furor erupted over this research, with some saying that reproductive technology had gone too far. Dr. Arthur Caplan, an ethicist then at the University of Minnesota, said that this kind of procreation upsets how society views the order of generations by creating grandmothers who were never mothers and mothers who never came into personhood. It puts the child in a difficult situation, arising from the fact that the mother was aborted, and it treats reproduction like a commodity. Said Caplan, "It is one thing to want a child, but there are limits. . . . It seems to me that no one should be able to create a child from your eggs or your sperm without your consent."[2] Dr. Robert Levine, of the Yale University School of Medicine, said that long-standing ethical principles forbid the use of a vulnerable population just because it is convenient. He said donors should be able and free to consent.[3]

But Dr. John Fletcher, an ethicist at the University of Virginia at Charlottesville, claims that we should also consider the pain and trouble to egg donors when considering new ways to acquire eggs. He does not think that being born by this method would cause significant emotional problems later on. Others also think it would be acceptable to use fetuses as a source of eggs.[4]

TEST-TUBE BABIES: PREGNANCY BEGINS IN THE LAB

The first test-tube baby was born in 1978 in England. Her mother's fallopian tubes were blocked, preventing a fertilized egg from reaching the uterus, where it could develop. In a widely publicized experiment, doctors surgically removed one of Mrs. Brown's eggs and fertilized it in a petri dish with her husband's sperm. The dish contained blood serum and nutrients that are needed for fertilization to progress. After a few days, the fertilized egg was implanted inside Mrs. Brown's uterus.

Since the conception did not take place *in vivo* (inside the body) but was *in vitro* (in the glass dish), it became known as in vitro fertilization (IVF). On July 25, Louise Brown was born, weighing five pounds, twelve ounces. A year later, test-tube twins were born in Australia; in 1981, the first IVF baby was born in America.

Of the three million infertile couples in America, about twenty thousand use IVF each year. Several eggs are taken from a woman's ovaries, placed in a lab dish and fertilized with sperm, then incubated. When they reach the embryo stage, doctors transfer them into the woman's uterus. IVF costs about $6,000 to $10,000 per treatment, and about 15 percent succeed. New methods are improving success rates. Doctors cut holes in the tough outer coating of the egg and insert sperm directly into it. As of 1994, more than three thousand IVF babies were being born each year in the United States, with one being born daily somewhere in the world.[5]

Unusual situations may arise. Using a procedure called embryonic transfer, a donor's eggs are fertilized, in a lab or in the donor. Then the embryo is transferred to another woman, perhaps the spouse of the sperm donor. Complications could occur if the donor decides she wants the child (which is genetically half hers) or if she decides not to have fertilized ova transferred.

The mere thought of egg banks and sperm banks alarms many people. Eggs and sperm from such sources could be used to produce children with no family foundation. An infertile woman could be implanted with the eggs of another woman that have been fertilized by sperm from the infertile woman's mate. This is called artificial embryonation. Or she could be implanted with another woman's egg that has been fertilized by a donor, then carry a baby whose genes do not match either hers or her mate's.

A scandal erupted in 1995 at a major fertility clinic in Irvine,

California. The clinic was shut down after more than a year of investigations following complaints that doctors had transferred fertilized eggs from one patient to another without permission. Doctors were also accused of conducting research without first obtaining informed consent and of using fertility drugs that had not yet been approved. About 1,900 frozen embryos were stored without an inventory so that some patients could not find out where their embryos had gone. The doctors denied any wrongdoing. Later, doctors were accused of actually stealing eggs from some women.

Calling these "serious charges," ethicist Dr. Arthur Caplan said, "You've got claims made of the improper use of embryos and eggs. You've got claims made that people were created under false pretenses. You've got claims made of research being done on vulnerable subjects—desperate couples who were infertile—without obtaining informed consent."[6]

Of this whole area of medicine, Dr. John Buster, a professor at the University of California, says, "It involves exchanging commodities that no one has ever exchanged before, and the ethics and morality and legal aspects of this thing are just not worked out yet because we've never done this before."[7]

THE DEBATE OVER IVF

Doctors have called the process of IVF "simple," but to many people, this matter is far from simple. Some conservative Christians view IVF as a way of "playing God" and tampering with human life in a lab. Catholic and Muslim leaders, along with Orthodox Jews, have also criticized the procedure, saying that it treats human beings like products, much like an automobile. They say embryos should be regarded as human beings, not mere biological material. IVF procedures tend to use more than one egg, to improve the odds for success. In the case of Mrs. Brown, more than one hundred attempts were made before IVF worked. Fertilized eggs that are not implanted are customarily discarded. To some people, this means ending human life that began at conception.

In addition, Catholic doctrine opposes artificial insemination and certain forms of birth control, as well as abortion. Since 1949, the Church has officially opposed procreation that takes place outside intercourse between married couples. The Church's position emphasizes the dignity of marriage and the importance of that relationship on the development of children.[8]

Some countries have banned IVF. In 1995, authorities in Warsaw, Poland, banned private fertility clinics from doing IVF procedures. They claim that it violates Poland's 1993 antiabortion laws (the strictest in Europe aside from Northern Ireland). Critics said that medical decisions should not be controlled by religious doctrine. Senator Zofia Kuratowska, a medical doctor, called IVF "a normal method in civilized countries."[9] Others pointed out that the World Health Organization classifies infertility as a social disease. Polish women who had hoped to receive IVF treatments were upset that the clinic was closed. Poland's medical ethics board agreed to consider this matter.

The U.S. government has received thousands of letters from scientists and others who oppose spending federal money on IVF research. Citizens say they resent contributing taxes to something they find morally wrong, an objection that has also been raised to federally funded abortions. Others say that IVF is not a proper use of health care resources or medical expertise. Here, they say, doctors are not treating or curing disease but are trying to help someone fulfill a desire. Leon Kass, a physician and ethical writer, says, "Just as infertility is not a disease, so providing a child by artificial means to a woman with blocked oviducts is not treatment. . . . What is being 'treated' is her desire—a perfectly normal and unobjectionable desire—to bear a child."[10]

Are some desires more worthy than others, especially when public funds pay all or part of the cost? Many insurance companies do not reimburse people for IVF treatments, viewing them as elective health care, not a need. Yet six states require insurers to pay for IVF.

Critics have asked whether the cost of IVF outweighs the benefits. A 1994 analysis conducted by Project Hope of Bethesda, Maryland, found that the average cost to society of producing each successful pregnancy through IVF was between $60,000 to $110,000.[11]

Those who oppose or have mixed feelings about IVF have urged scientists to focus instead on the root causes of infertility. Finding and correcting these would allow conception and pregnancy to go forward on its own and not require doctors to take such active roles in producing a child or a certain kind of child.[12]

Supporters of IVF say that one of the main goals of medicine is to relieve human suffering (the ethical principle of nonmaleficence), including the psychological pain of those who cannot bear a child. Other health care aims to help people attain desires or overcome limitations, such as poor vision or the loss of a limb. People who desire sleep can receive medications. A 1980 Gallup Poll showed that Americans favored the use of IVF by a margin of two to one. More than half said they would try IVF themselves if this were the only way in which they could have children.[13]

Opponents of IVF warn that humans are on dangerous ground when they manipulate life this way. Tinkering with conception and birth could harm humankind's self-image and, once begun, anything is possible. This is a "slippery slope" argument—the idea that once begun, events gain momentum and cannot be kept under control.

Author Samuel Gorovitz says this might not happen, depending upon how each policy is defined and justified: "If IVF research on embryos is justified by the principle that prenatal fetal life is of no moral importance, there will be no basis for restraint in regard to research on later-stage fetuses. So it can matter decisively how the justification of first steps is formulated."[14]

People continue to debate what should be done with fertilized embryos created outside the body. At present, most are destroyed, but some are frozen. A Roman Catholic archbishop, Sir Frank Little, said, "The embryo must be regarded as a person, never as an object. Is the dignity of the human person fully expressed, and adequately safeguarded, in the so-called test-tube production of human life?"[15]

For years, the strains of certain types of laboratory animals have been preserved through freezing embryos. Human embryos that have developed to the six- to eight-cell stage—smaller than a grain of salt—can also be frozen, to be implanted in a uterus later on.

Legal battles have arisen over frozen embryos. In a 1994 divorce case, a couple debated whether five frozen embryos were "children" and therefore they had to file motions for "custody," or whether the embryos should be viewed as property. The embryos developed after Maureen and Steven Kass, a Long Island couple, tried IVF in May 1993. When the couple decided to divorce, Mrs. Kass wanted to keep the embryos and have them implanted so that she could give birth. Mr. Kass wanted them to be destroyed.

Mrs. Kass said that, as a Catholic, she disagreed. She said, "They are already fertilized. That's a potential for life. They should not be destroyed because he changed his mind." She also said that she had gone through a great deal in order to acquire the embryos.[16] In 1995, a New York court ruled in favor of Mrs. Kass, who stated that she would use them in the hopes of bearing a child.

Should Mrs. Kass go on to give birth, Mr. Kass would probably be required to financially support any children. He complained that his wife, who had filed for the divorce, was now forcing him into an unfair situation. "I'm being held hostage until I do what they want. It's unconscionable. . . . They [the embryos] are just two cells. . . . They are not even attached to a uterus yet."[17]

In a Tennessee case a few years earlier, the state's supreme court awarded frozen embryos to the ex-husband, who had them destroyed. But in that case, the ex-wife wanted to donate the embryos to an infertile couple rather than use them herself. The Tennessee court did say, however, that fertilized embryos could be used over the objection of one party if there were "no reasonable alternative" to bringing about a pregnancy.[18]

As situations like these arise, the uses of frozen embryos continue to raise bioethical concerns. Critics fear that in time, frozen embryos could be offered for sale, like commercial products.

BIRTH AFTER MENOPAUSE

How old is too old to give birth? Men have fathered children in their sixties, or even beyond. Yet the age limit for adoptive mothers is usually forty-five. In 1994, an Englishwoman gave birth to twins at age fifty-nine, although she had already gone through menopause—the ending of menstrual periods and fertility. She became pregnant when donor eggs were fertilized with her husband's sperm and implanted into her uterus. Then she took hormones during pregnancy. A sixty-one-year-old Italian woman also bore a child through this process.

The doctor at a Rome clinic who performed this procedure has been criticized. English doctors had refused to do the procedure, saying that a fifty-nine-year-old woman was too old to face the emotional stress of child-rearing. Virginia Bottomley, the British Secretary of Health, said, "Women do not have the right to have a child. The child has the right to a suitable home."[19] Other critics said that children of older mothers might grow up fearing their mothers will die before they grow up. They called the pregnancies a wrongful tampering with the stages of life and said the women were exercising selfish desires to have babies out of season.

Others disagreed. An editorial in the *New York Times* said

that youth does not guarantee a suitable home and that older parents may even be more capable. Many grandmothers rear children quite well, and women often live to their eighties and nineties these days. When older men father children and die a few years later, people seldom express dismay about the fate of those children.

The Rome clinic required the older mothers to pass physical and psychological tests, be nonsmokers, and have a life expectancy of twenty years or more, based on age and family history. Authors Bonnie Steinbock and Ron McClamrock claim, "So long as a woman is emotionally and physically equipped to be a reasonably good mother, there is no reason why age should be an absolute barrier for women any more than it is for men."[20]

Dr. Mark Siegler, director of the Center for Medical Clinical Ethics at the University of Chicago, contends, "To say that simply because these women are post-menopausal and above the age of 50 that they can't provide adequate child care to a baby, that is patently ridiculous. There is this sense that we know better than they do what's best for them and that would be to act their age."[21] The American Medical Association's Council on Ethical and Judicial Affairs emphasizes the principle of autonomy, saying that each case should be decided by the woman, with the advice of her doctor.

REPRODUCTION AFTER DEATH

In January 1995, a baby girl was born in Italy. The egg that gave rise to this child came from a woman who had died in 1993. The story began in 1992, when the woman and her husband asked doctors to help them conceive a child. At a fertility clinic, eight human embryos were developed from the couple's egg and sperm cells by means of in vitro fertilization. Four embryos were implanted in the woman, but each pregnancy failed; four remained frozen at the time of her death. The husband asked the doctor to implant them in his thirty-three-year-old sister. One embryo developed. Under Italian law, the resulting baby girl belonged to the birth mother and her husband, so the natural father adopted the baby.

In the wake of this birth, Roman Catholic leaders and others demanded that the government ban certain kinds of reproductive methods, including IVF, and implantations of fertilized embryos. Critics called the situation immoral and incestuous, because of the relationship between the father and the birth mother. A poll of Italian citizens showed that 52 percent found this "morally unacceptable," while 18 percent approved. Church leaders said that all embryos are people and destroying any of them was murder. Former archbishop Ersilio Cardinal Tonini criticized doctors for "sacrificing seven human beings, to produce just one."[22]

Should technology be used to fertilize eggs outside the human body? Should a fertilized embryo *ever* be destroyed once it is created? Is it proper to use the eggs or sperm of a deceased person after she or he has died? What if the person requested it? Both women and men can now become "parents" after death. When a woman has left behind frozen embryos, they can be implanted into another woman and carried to term. Sperm that is removed quickly after death can be kept for an indefinite period of time, frozen at a temperature of -321°F.

In 1994, after Pam Maresca's husband, Manny, died in an automobile accident two weeks after their marriage, she asked that some of his sperm be removed and frozen before he was buried. The Floridian said that she planned to use it to conceive a baby at some later time. Her late husband's family approved.[23]

In other cases, the sperm of a deceased man has been used for conception. Music teacher Nancy Hart gave birth to a daughter in 1991, using the sperm of her husband, who had died months earlier. Legal conflicts arose when the state of Louisiana refused to recognize the child as her father's natural daughter, since she was conceived after his death. In 1994, Nancy Hart filed a lawsuit to have her daughter declared Edward Hart's legitimate child and heir and to claim survivors' Social Security benefits, given to minor children after a parent dies. Supporting Hart's position, an attorney at the Center for Reproductive Law and Policy in New York City said that laws need to change to reflect the new ways that people can reproduce.[24] In 1995 a judge ruled that the child is her father's legal child. She was also deemed eligible for his Social Security benefits.

Can reproductive materials be bequeathed in a will? California courts faced this issue during the early 1990s. A Los Angeles lawyer had willed frozen sperm to the woman he lived with before his death so that she could be artificially inseminated. His grown children sought to prevent the woman from receiving the sperm. They argued that fathering children after death was "egotistic and irresponsible." They also claimed that the birth of such children would bring emotional and financial stress to the family, since any new children would share the man's estate.[25] The California Supreme Court allowed the bequest, overruling a superior court judge who had ruled that the sperm be destroyed.

CHOOSING WHO WILL BE BORN

"It's a boy!" or "It's a girl!" are announcements once heard only after the birth of a baby. These days, expectant parents can learn the sex of a child in advance, along with a great deal of genetic information, as discussed in chapter 3.

Since abortion is legal, a woman or a couple can choose to end a pregnancy because they want a child of a different sex. A number of physicians refuse to perform such abortions, but it is not always possible to find out a patient's true motives.

In China, a 1994 law bans sex-screening of fetuses. Doctors who do sex screenings may lose their licenses. The Chinese have traditionally preferred sons, who bring economic support to the family. But for several decades, the Communist government required people to limit their families to one child. Many people aborted girl fetuses or killed infant girls, leading to an imbalance in the number of males to females in China. Author Jane Stein says, "Preference for male children is virtually a global desire. It is estimated that there would be a 20 percent excess of male births if all parents had their way. The implications of this—ethical, economic, cultural, sociological—are enormous."[26]

The 1994 law also requires Chinese women to have abortions when screening shows a serious genetic defect. People who have been diagnosed with conditions that would keep their offspring from being able to live independently are banned from marrying. An international human rights organization criticized this law, which seems to promote forced abortions and sterilizations, an infringement of a woman's autonomy.[27]

LIMITS ON REPRODUCTIVE FREEDOM

People around the world have expressed outrage that, during World War II, Nazi Germany implemented policies of eugenics. As part of their plan to "improve" the human race, the Nazis sterilized people who had physical or mental disabilities or other "undesirable" traits. Forced sterilizations have been done elsewhere, too. As late as 1927, in the case *Buck v. Bell* the U.S. Supreme Court ruled such operations legal if certain requirements were first met. People judged to be insane or imbeciles could be sterilized without their consent. In Virginia, thousands of institutionalized women were sterilized, many of whom were only mildly disabled.

Is it ethical to prevent mentally incompetent people from having children or to force them to terminate a pregnancy? Some courts have upheld sterilization of women who were not capable of caring for children. Parents have asked courts to authorize the sterilization of a mentally handicapped child.

The legal system has also considered the ethics of sterilizing men who chronically commit rape or molest children. Some courts have sought to give such criminals a choice of jail time or either surgery or drugs that will eliminate the sex drive. These proposals have been quite controversial and were ruled unconstitutional in state courts.

In recent years, courts have wrestled with the issue of whether pregnant women can be legally forced to abstain from behaviors that could harm an unborn child. Child abuse statutes have been invoked for this purpose. Can the use of drugs or alcohol or smoking during pregnancy be viewed as a form of child abuse? They may result in birth defects and mental and physical handicaps. A child whose mother abuses cocaine or heroin can be born addicted and suffer pain and other symptoms, as well as brain damage.

During the 1980s, a California district attorney charged a woman with a misdemeanor after she disobeyed a court warning not to use drugs. Her baby was born with defects and died six weeks later, with traces of amphetamine in his blood. She was charged with failure to follow medical advice leading to her child's death and failure to provide adequate care. The penalty for a conviction would be a fine and one year in jail.[28] The National Right to Life Committee supported this action. Others disagreed, saying that pregnant women should not be captive to medical rules. The Reproductive Freedom Project of the American Civil Liberties Union (ACLU) opposed "shifting rights" from a pregnant woman to a fetus.

In Youngstown, Ohio, a judge ordered that a woman have her fallopian tubes tied, a reversible surgical procedure that prevents conception. The woman, a crack addict, had four children by different fathers. She had failed in several rehabilitation programs and was not caring for her children. The court order would force her to undergo an invasive medical procedure. Should her right to make her own decision (autonomy) take precedence over the right of a baby to a healthy life (nonmaleficence)?

Related questions arise when women have AIDS, since there

is a 15 to 30 percent chance of passing the virus to an unborn child. Should laws forbid women with AIDS from getting pregnant? What penalties could be imposed?

These issues involve conflicts between, on the one hand, the rights of a society to define the social good and, on the other hand, individual privacy and freedom. Supporters of penalizing women in these kinds of cases have said that some mistakes are so repetitive and grievous that those who make them must give up certain freedoms.

SURROGATE MOTHERS

Some infertile women, or those who have health problems that make pregnancy unwise, turn to surrogates. A surrogate—substitute—agrees for financial or humanitarian reasons to bear a child for someone else. The baby may be conceived by IVF using the couple's egg and sperm, or the surrogate mother may conceive with her own egg and the father's sperm, via artificial insemination.

Surrogacy may have existed for thousands of years and is mentioned in the Bible. It drew public attention in the United States in 1980, when a woman using the pseudonym Elizabeth Kane was artificially inseminated with a man's sperm and relinquished the child to him and his wife, signing away all parental rights.

The case stirred controversy, with critics calling Mrs. Kane a "baby-seller," since she had received money. Opponents said that it demeaned human dignity to treat babies as commodities. Some lawmakers called for a ban on all surrogate contracts, saying they were patently immoral. Even so, ads for surrogates continued to appear in newspapers and magazines. In some cases, female friends or family members agreed to serve as surrogates.

Some institutions arrange surrogacy contracts. The Infertility Center, founded in 1976, was involved in the highly controversial "Baby M." surrogacy case during the 1980s. Mary Beth Whitehead had been artificially inseminated with the sperm of William Stern, then carried a baby for him and his wife, Elizabeth. After the birth, Whitehead said she was emotionally unable to give up the baby.

A court case ensued as the Sterns demanded that Whitehead honor the contract she had signed. During the case, details of that contract became public. It specified that the Infertility Center would collect a $7,500 fee, up front. Whitehead would receive no money if anything happened to her or the baby, such as a miscarriage. In addition, Whitehead had to undergo amniocentesis to check the condition of the fetus; if defects were found, she was to have an abortion and would receive $1,000. If she delivered a healthy infant to the Sterns, she would receive $10,000. "Can any contract to buy or to sell a human being be valid?" asked an editorial writer in the *Commonweal*.[29] Philosophy professor Gerald F. Kreyche commented that it was ludicrous to describe a surrogate as selling a service rather than a product—the baby.[30]

In the custody battle, the judge ruled that Baby M. was the legal child of Whitehead and William Stern, her genetic parents. He awarded custody to the Sterns, saying that would be in the child's best interests. Whitehead received visitation rights. She later sued the Infertility Center, claiming she had not been screened well enough before she signed the surrogacy contract, and won an out-of-court settlement of several thousand dollars.

Since 1976, more than 10,000 babies have been born in America under surrogacy arrangements, usually for fees ranging from $10,000 to $17,000. About the same amount goes to the agency-broker. Courts, legislatures, and policy-makers have differing views about surrogacy contracts. Some states have banned them. About twelve others, including Indiana, consider such contracts unenforceable or limit the fees surrogates may collect. New Hampshire and Virginia permit only married couples to enter into surrogacy contracts.

Most centers screen surrogate mothers, but few conduct thorough evaluations of those who will receive the baby. A 1995 case shows the potential problems. Through the Infertility Center, a single man, James Alan Austin, paid an Indiana woman $30,000 to bear a child for him by artificial insemination. On January 8, he took the five-week-old boy to a hospital, where he died. Admitting he had beaten the infant, Austin was charged with manslaughter.

After the baby was admitted to the hospital, the birth mother flew to Pennsylvania to reclaim him if he survived. Later, she handled funeral arrangements. Austin's lawyer claimed that his client had no parenting skills and that the Infertility Center had failed in a duty to prepare him for parenthood.[31]

Law professor Lori Andrews, an expert on surrogacy, comments, "This case points up the whole debate about whether surrogacy should come under the adoption model, with intensive screening of the home the child is going to, or the biological reproduction model, under which there's no screening."[32]

People continue to ask many questions about surrogacy: Who is the legal mother? What happens if the birth mother changes her mind about giving up the child? Can the child have a legal relationship with both mothers? Who is responsible to register the birth and support the child? Could the child claim any inheritance rights in regard to the surrogate? What if the couple dies before the birth? What if the couple decides they can no longer raise a child, due to financial changes or divorce? All of these situations have arisen.

One of the most sensitive issues is what happens if the child is born with handicaps. In some cases, contracts specify that the future parents will accept only a "healthy baby." Along those lines, some future parents seek to control the behavior of the surrogate during pregnancy to ensure a healthy child.

In a case featured on a segment of the *Phil Donahue Show*, a surrogate mother admitted that she had had intercourse with her husband during the same week she was artificially inseminated. After the baby was born, handicapped, the couples argued about who should raise him. Paternity tests showed that the surrogate's husband was the child's father, so the surrogate kept the child.

To many people, surrogacy is another sign of the decline in values and is demeaning to marriage, the family, and sexual intimacy. They say that, like reproductive technology, surrogacy further separates sex and love from reproduction. Some feminists argue that using women's bodies as human incubators or baby-making machines is degrading. Also, surrogates tend to be poorer women engaged by wealthier ones. But a surrogate who admits she carried two babies for the money said that she preferred this to other jobs she could have held at the time. Surrogates have said they have the right to make such contracts with other consenting adults.

Some surrogates enjoy bringing children into the world and helping others to have a family. One woman said, "I have three children and I had such easy pregnancies. I enjoy being pregnant, but my husband and I don't want to raise any more children. This way, I gave somebody a precious, irreplaceable gift."

■　　■　　■

Reproductive options are advancing all the time, especially since some are financed by independent, private facilities. As a society, we will have to weigh the costs and benefits and decide whether and how to regulate these developments.

FIVE

The Dilemmas of Research

L.R. experiences dangerous side-effects from the medication that controls his mental illness. While he was mentally competent, he consented to test a new drug with fewer side-effects. Two days into the experiment, while experiencing acute psychotic symptoms, L.R. demanded to end the test. Should his request be granted, since people have the right to leave an experiment, or should doctors assume he would want them to honor his earlier decision?

■

Research on human embryos may yield important new findings about health and disease. The government recently approved research on very early embryos. Should experiments be reserved for embryos that were not implanted after in vitro fertilization or should scientists also create embryos expressly for research?

At the heart of ethical issues surrounding research is the fact that it is usually conducted in order to benefit many people, not necessarily those who are research subjects. Therefore, the rights of human subjects must be diligently protected. Says ethicist Bette-Jane Crigger, "It becomes especially important to assure that subjects are fully informed of the possible benefits and risks of research and freely consent to participate. So, too, subjects must be chosen equitably so that the benefits and burdens of research do not fall disproportionately to particular individuals or groups."[1] Crigger is among those who believe that since the community stands to benefit at the expense of a few, people can collect financial and other assistance if they have been harmed by an experiment.

In order to sort out the bioethical issues involving research, Joseph Fletcher suggests that we consider these factors:

- risk (to subjects or investigators)
- avoidance of harm (nonmaleficence)
- reportage (professional integrity)
- prehuman tests (on other organisms insofar as possible)
- consent
- benefit
- avoidance of deception (of subjects)
- design (scientific standards)
- privacy (confidentiality)
- motivation of participants (subjects and investigators)
- cost (as part of risk-benefit analysis)
- fraud (deception in reporting)
- in-course cancellation (by subjects or investigators)
- monitoring
- review (peer or public)[2]

DEVELOPMENT OF RESEARCH ETHICS

Treatment of human research subjects has often been insensitive, careless, even cruel. Murderous "experiments" were conducted by Nazi doctors on concentration camp inmates during World War II. People endured injections of dyes in their eyes, lethal doses of bacteria, cyanide injections into the heart, and live dissections. Many died; others were left sterile or disabled.

Hearing about these events at the Nuremberg trials, the international community was moved to develop careful, detailed guidelines for experimentation on human beings. The Nuremberg Code states that scientists should base their experiments on the results of animal testing and thorough knowledge of the natural history of the disease or problem under study. The anticipated results must justify the performance of the experiment. Experiments also must be conducted in proper facilities in ways that avoid unnecessary physical and mental suffering and injury. They should not be done if it seems likely that death or disabling injury will occur. Those conducting research need to be well qualified and should use the highest degree of skill and care during every stage. Subjects should be free to quit if their physical or mental state makes continuation seem impossible. In essence, the experiment must be ethical from the onset, with a reasonable chance for success. Scientists must anticipate any harmful results and determine that the potential benefits outweigh the actual and potential risks.[3]

Later, the Helsinki Declaration of the World Medical Association echoed these principles. The code and declaration stress that subjects be fully informed and give voluntary consent.

In 1974, after reviewing problems in research practices, the U.S. Department of Health, Education, and Welfare developed its own regulations. A system of committees, the Institutional Review Boards, reviews research proposals to make sure they comply with these regulations. The IRBs can ban a particular study, require changes in its design, or monitor it.

INFORMED CONSENT

What constitutes informed consent? A person must be mentally competent, capable of understanding the information, and aware of the full nature of the experiment and its risks. Informed consent also respects the right of competent adults to accept or reject health care, based on their personal values and goals.[4]

Surveys of Americans from all walks of life indicate they value informed consent regarding their health care.[5] This idea dates back to ancient times, when limits were placed on physicians. In the Anglo-American tradition, the law of trespass covered nonconsensual medical treatment that involved some type of harm or offensive touching or treatment of a patient.

Difficulties with informed consent can arise when people are not mentally competent or are minors. Some states provide for the appointment of guardians or advocates who try to determine the best interests of such persons. When individuals have periods of acute mental illness, but are sometimes mentally sound, they may be able to designate such an advocate themselves. They may also be able to spell out, in specific and detailed terms, under what conditions they would want their opinions to be overruled if they were acutely mentally ill and unable to make rational decisions.

THE TUSKEGEE EXPERIMENTS

An experiment that violated the principle of informed consent and other ethical principles took place from 1932 into the 1950s in Alabama. The Tuskegee Project, as it was called, was financed and run by the federal government. Signs advertised for "colored" men to come to Tuskegee Institute for medical care.

More than seven hundred men became involved, all illiterate or semiliterate. They did not receive information nor were they told that they were part of a study. Public health officials at the clinic told the men what to do. Nurses administered tests for syphilis, a sexually transmitted disease that can cause serious symptoms or can lay dormant, with no apparent symptoms. Researchers wanted to know what would happen if syphilis remained untreated during a person's lifetime, studying the outcome after death by means of autopsies.

Test results were not shared with the participants, although many already had syphilis. Many of the men thought they were receiving medical treatment. In fact, an Alabama law at that time required that anyone who had syphilis must be treated. More than three hundred men died. Others healed and their disease became dormant. Death could have been prevented with treatment.

By the 1990s, only twenty of the men were still alive. Civil rights attorney Fred Gray filed a class-action suit on behalf of the Tuskegee group and won a $10 million settlement, which was divided among survivors and the families of those who had died, amounting to between $17,000 and $35,000 apiece. During Senate hearings on the Tuskegee case, Senator Edward Kennedy (D-Mass.) introduced legislation that forbids researchers to deny vital medical treatment to human subjects who have a known disease.

RADIATION EXPERIMENTS

During 1993 and 1994, information from previously classified files showed that, from the 1940s into the 1960s, the U.S. government had conducted secret experiments in which people were exposed to radioactive materials. Tests were conducted on terminally ill people, army personnel, pregnant women, stillborn infants and aborted fetuses, mentally retarded children, prisoners, and others. This was one outgrowth of the Manhattan Project, which was formed to build atomic bombs during World War II. Thousands of workers were handling radioactive materials. The Atomic Energy Commission (AEC) and scientists wondered how the radiation could affect humans, so a number of experiments followed:

- Between 1945 and 1947, eighteen patients who had terminal illnesses were injected with plutonium. Scientists planned to track the rate at which plutonium was excreted from their bodies.

- In 1953, Project Sunshine aimed to find out what would happen to people, animals, and plants that were exposed to radioactive fallout from atmospheric tests of nuclear weapons. In one test, radioactive iodine-131 was given to pregnant women who were about to have abortions in order to study the effects on the fetus.
- At nuclear testing sites in the Southwest and elsewhere, army personnel were exposed to radiation from atomic explosions. There were 215 atmospheric nuclear tests between 1945 and 1963, five of them underwater. Between 1963 and 1992, the United States conducted 1,149 nuclear tests, far more than were reported at the time. Many veterans later developed cancer and other illnesses that they attributed to their exposure.
- During the 1970s, researchers halted a program in which airplanes had been flown through radioactive exhaust from nuclear rockets in order to measure the doses to air crews.

By the seventies, reports about radiation experiments began circulating. As people sought more detailed information, officials at the U.S. Department of Energy (DOE) promised to look into the matter. Early in 1994, President Bill Clinton told all federal agencies to check their files for radiation experiments. He appointed the Advisory Committee on Human Radiation Experiments.

When the DOE set up a hotline for victims of the experiments, it received thousands of calls. On June 4, 1994, Hazel O'Leary, secretary of the DOE, said that the agency had already discovered forty-eight radiation experiments on human subjects; by 1995, that number surpassed one thousand. Victims' organizations were formed throughout America, and lawsuits were filed to aid victims and their families.

In defense of the experiments, the scientists involved claimed that the standards for conducting research were not as strict in the past as they are today. However, the Clinton Advisory Committee found that in 1942, when early experiments were conducted, a government committee had recommended that all research subjects be fully informed about the nature and risks of the tests. In 1947, the AEC had said that humans involved in any experiments should understand and consent to them. At least two doctors were supposed to certify, in writing, that a patient knew the nature and risks of the treatment or test and had consented. Also in 1947, the AEC said that any testing done must be likely to have a therapeutic effect. By then, the Pentagon had adopted the Nuremberg Code to safeguard human subjects' rights and safety.

In 1993, at one of six congressional hearings held to discuss ethical abuses in the radiation experiments, Senator Jeff Bingaman of New Mexico said, "It's an unbelievable story, quite frankly, to think that we would have a program that used human beings to experiment in this way."[6] The publicity alerted Americans to the need for continuing vigilance into research standards and practices.

EMBRYO RESEARCH

More recently, people have debated whether or not research should be conducted on fetuses or embryos. There are two main types of fetal research: basic (studying reproductive biology and fetal growth and development) and therapeutic (seeking knowledge about infertility, birth defects, and disease). The benefits of such research are viewed as potentially great, perhaps reducing the incidence of babies born with severe mental and/or physical handicaps. Without studying embryos, scientists must rely on collecting statistics and gathering information that may not be available, standardized, or accurate.

Research using fetal tissue increased during the 1950s, when this research was used in the development of the polio vaccine and techniques of prenatal screening. During the 1970s, the National Institutes of Health began to fund embryo research. After President Ronald Reagan was elected in 1980, he supported a ban on federal funding of research using fetal tissue from elective abortions.

President Bush continued this ban but allowed federal funding of such research when the fetal tissue was obtained after a spontaneous abortion—one that occurs on its own—or ectopic pregnancy, a dangerous condition in which a fertilized egg implants and begins to grow in a woman's fallopian tube. The ban did not permit federal funding of fetal tissue transplant studies, either.

In September 1994, a panel of experts including scientists, ethicists, and lawyers suggested that the government fund research on human embryos. They said that an embryo does not have the same moral or legal status as a living infant or child and that many are discarded. At about one week old, an embryo is known as a blastocyst and can fit on the point of a needle. At fourteen days, the point at which such research would no longer be permitted, it is a clump of cells about the size of a period. At this point, most cells will go on to form the placental tissue rather than organs. At eight weeks, the group of cells is known as a fetus.

Should the embryos left over from IVF that are not used to produce pregnancy be available for research? Scientists argue that discarding them destroys an opportunity to advance knowledge that could help people. These early embryos could be nurtured and exposed to various environmental influences to find out what happens. More controversial is a proposal to create embryos in the lab expressly for research. After using research embryos, scientists could destroy them.

Supporting this idea in an editorial for the *New York Times* Philip M. Boffey wrote, "Those who think of the embryo as human life will no doubt oppose its use in any research from which it does not benefit. But others like me will find it hard to consider the tiny clump of primitive cells as anything approaching a 'person.' Yes, the clump has the genetic heritage to develop into a full person. But it has no sense of self, no awareness, no feeling, no nervous system, no organs of any kind. At 14 days it is no bigger than the period at the end of this sentence."[7]

Critics worry that researchers may manipulate life-forms for trivial reasons. They think embryos are entitled to continued life, are innocent, helpless, and may experience pain and suffering. The research does not benefit them in any way. The Vatican said that research with an embryo is not acceptable "were it to involve risk to the embryo's physical integrity or life." It is not the researcher's place to decide who shall live and who will die.[8]

Clearly, an embryo cannot give informed consent to be the object of research. "Each human being has the right to be regarded as one who cannot rightfully be subordinated to that society or to any person within it," says W. E. May.[9] May says that it is not ethical for an embryo to be subject to decisions made by others. Yet parents often give consent when medical procedures are performed on their children.

Ethicist Joseph Fletcher has said that research with embryos or fetuses may be ethical, depending on the clinical situation. He says that scientists could decide it is proper to conduct studies on fetal material that has come from voluntary or therapeutic abortions. A decision would have to made as to whether consent must first be obtained from the woman. Fletcher says that fetal tissue research might be conducted in the uterus, if there is maternal consent, and even with live fetuses in utero if there is no substantial risk to the fetus and both mother and father consent. In these cases, the parties must be fully informed.[10]

LAWS REGARDING EMBRYO RESEARCH

In response to these kinds of issues, Congress considered laws to prevent changes in methods of abortion, regulate payment for fetal tissues, and ban women from designating tissue for donation. Late in 1994, the National Institutes of Health issued guidelines on the use of human embryos in research. They stated that embryos do not have "the same moral status as infants and children"[11] and that in their early stages, they have no possibility of sensing or feeling pain. A committee made up of eighteen scientists, lawyers, ethicists, and citizens met and read thousands of documents as well as heard the pros and cons from many experts while debating the bioethics of embryo research.

They considered how other nations have dealt with this type of research: Germany and a few other countries ban it, while Great Britain allows it under certain circumstances. Cloning research was deemed not permissible, and the use of embryos after the fourteenth day was also troublesome, since that is the point at which the primitive streak begins to appear—a structure that is destined to develop into the central nervous system. The committee strictly banned experimental manipulation of an embryo growing inside a woman's body and implanting any embryos that had been genetically or chemically manipulated in a lab. Scientists would be barred from making human-animal combinations or cloning one embryo into two, creating identical human twins.

The most hotly debated topic was the creation of some embryos under "compelling circumstances." This could be done in order to learn more about the process of fertilization, something scientists cannot study in embryos that are already formed. Scientists would also be allowed to place a new nucleus into an egg for the purposes of learning how to correct inherited defects.

Most embryos for research come from unused IVF programs. Some ethicists say that since these embryos are usually discarded, it is more ethical to use them in research than throw them away. John Fletcher, who supports some of this research, points out that children with cancer are often given experimental treatments. "It does a terrible disservice to these children if we expect them to take part in cancer research and then we shy away from doing the embryo experiments necessary to understand how their cancers began," says Fletcher.[12]

GENETIC RESEARCH

The National Institutes of Health has set up a fifteen-member advisory panel to make decisions involving recombinant DNA technology. The committee determines whether to approve any proposals involving gene therapy. In addition, the FDA must approve research studies involving gene therapy.

A recent situation shows how research proposals are evaluated. In 1994, scientists were permitted to try gene therapy for blocked blood vessels. They planned to add cells containing genes near blocked arteries in patients' legs in order to promote the growth of new vessels around the blockage. The advisory committee noted that the risk of serious complications from this therapy was below 10 percent. Subjects would be patients who were not candidates for surgery and who could be helped only by this procedure.

EXPERIMENTAL TREATMENT

During the 1990s, the National Surgical Adjuvant Breast and Bowel Project (NSABBP) ran an experiment involving some 11,000 healthy women at high risk for breast cancer. The women agreed to take a drug called tamoxifen in a trial study to see if it prevented cancer later on. As part of this study, the women were carefully screened, had numerous physical examinations, and were required to sign informed-consent forms and waivers, explaining possible side effects, such as blood clots, eye problems, and slight risks of both liver cancer and uterine cancer.

The experiment has been criticized by those who believe tamoxifen is too dangerous to be given to healthy women for this purpose. After a woman in the study died of uterine cancer, Dr. Gail Greendale, who analyzed tamoxifen studies done in Europe, had the consent forms revised to show a greater risk of uterine cancer. She and some other researchers insisted upon more frequent cancer screenings, but patients were not monitored carefully at some of the research centers. Critics complained that risks were downplayed.

In 1994, the National Cancer Institute said that the study might prevent 132 cases of breast cancer but cause 83 cases of endometrial cancer and other problems. The trial went on in most places, but with new safeguards. Some women chose to continue even after being told that the risks were greater than was first thought.

The NSABBP decided to implement new policies to protect those who volunteer for research studies. An independent safety and monitoring board was established to provide ongoing protection to subjects and to halt any study that seems to involve new risks.[13]

Charles Weijer has proposed ethical guidelines for testing new drugs on healthy subjects: The drug ought to be relatively safe and free from life-threatening side effects, the subjects should be drawn from a population that is clearly at risk for the disease, the risk factors should be well understood, and the drug must stand on its own merits and be appropriate for the purpose involved in the study.[14] He criticizes the tamoxifen study on all four counts.

Like most other cancer research, breast cancer research emphasizes new drugs and treatments, paying far less attention to prevention. Since the 1960s, survival rates for breast cancer have remained about the same. The ratio of treatment to prevention research is about twenty to one. Critics of this ratio want to see more studies about how environment and lifestyle influence this disease.

LEARNING MEDICAL TECHNIQUES

At many teaching hospitals, doctors learn techniques by practicing on the bodies of people who have just died. These procedures include the insertion of tracheal tubes into the throat, inserting needles into the liver, and open-heart massage.

Most hospitals do not ask the grieving family's permission, feeling that it would upset them. Ethicists question this practice but acknowledge the dilemma. For the public good, doctors need experience in medical procedures, preferably with human subjects. Yet using bodies without permission can be viewed as immoral. Some hospitals handle the situation by including a consent for this type of activity in the forms people sign when they arrive for care.

Dr. George Kanoti, chairman of bioethics at Case Western Reserve in Cleveland, Ohio, says, "One of the greatest ethical dilemmas is the tension between individual rights and freedom and social good. And that's exactly what we're talking about here. Sometimes a compromise of an individual right may be necessary for a social good."[15]

■   ■   ■

The need for research or educational experiences using human subjects is often critical in order to permit learning and new and more effective treatments. But ethics demands that we address the goals of research or educational procedures, their limitations, and the safeguards and regulations that will apply.

S I X

The Question of Transplants

A fifty-year-old accident victim dies shortly after arriving at the hospital. The man has an organ donor card, but his brother, the next of kin, does not want any organs removed for transplantation. What should doctors do? Should living relatives be able to overrule the wishes of a deceased person to donate organs?

■

Two patients are good matches for a liver that has become available for transplant at a Florida hospital. One, a U.S. citizen, has no health insurance or money to pay for treatment. The other, a foreign citizen, has the money for a transplant, which is not available in his country. Who should receive the liver?

Organ transplantation is a dramatic example of how medical science can save lives and raise ethical questions. Scientists have been refining techniques for transplanting organs since the first transplant was done in 1954, using the kidney of a patient's identical twin. In the 1960s, surgeons successfully transplanted hearts and livers. At first, there was a high rate of rejection. The immune system regards such organs as foreign tissue and builds antibodies against them. For that reason, the organs of close relatives were used. Immunosuppressive drugs to inhibit the production of antibodies appeared in the 1960s, with improved versions in the late 1970s. By taking these drugs the rest of their lives, patients have a good chance to avoid organ rejection.

By 1995, surgeons could transplant most organs from a donor's body into that of a recipient. Heart, liver, lung, skin, cornea and kidney transplants were routine. Bone marrow transplants were being used to treat certain cancers and immune system disorders.

Although survival rates are higher than ever before, there are also more people awaiting organs. There have always been shortages, with more than 36,000 people waiting for organs as of 1994 and 4,300 newcomers each year. The General Accounting Office (GAO) reported that between 1988 and 1993, more than 10,000 people died for want of a transplant. Nearly half of all children awaiting organ transplants die before receiving them.

ETHICAL CONCERNS

The shortage of organ donors poses a major problem: Who will be chosen to receive organs that are in limited supply? A number of other issues arise, affecting health care professionals, patients, and the rest of society as potential donors and recipients.

The Code of Ethics of the Transplantation Society, an international group of physicians, states that transplanted organs from cadavers—dead persons—are preferable to those from live donors. This reduces risks to the living donor, who will have to live on with one kidney, for example.

One major section of the code discusses how to define death. This is paramount when a potential donor appears to be dying and a recipient desperately needs an organ. When shall the donor be declared dead or beyond recovery? The Transplantation Society made brain death, not cardiac (heart) death, the deciding factor. The code says that two physicians must verify death has occurred and that both of them must have some responsibility for the donor, not the person who would receive an organ. The physicians who determine death also should not be involved with the transplantation team.

A private, contract agency called the United Network for Organ Sharing coordinates services in the United States that are carried out by regional and individual transplant centers. This agency is monitored by the Department of Health and Human Services and uses a computer network to help match donors and recipients. Patients must meet several requirements in order to be considered a transplant candidate: They must be in danger of dying without a transplant; must not have medical conditions that make a transplant unfeasible; must be willing to take part in the medical procedures involved; and must have funds to pay for treatment, through private or public insurance or with personal funds. Age is also a factor, as patients older than their mid-seventies are seldom considered.

In determining who will receive a specific organ that becomes available, physicians look for a good match between donor and recipient, using a six-point antigen matching system. Antigens are substances in the blood that prompt the immune system to make antibodies. The closer the match is to six, the higher the chance for success. Antigens are genetically determined, so when members of certain racial or ethnic groups seldom donate organs, there are fewer matches for members of that group who need a transplant.

COST FACTORS

When seeking a transplant, a person who lacks health insurance must make a down payment, on average, of about $120,000 for American citizens or $250,000 for foreign nationals. The prices charged for organ transplants vary from one place to another. An article in the June 1993 issue of *Journal of the American Medical Association* analyzed transplants for the year 1988 and found that charges to procure kidneys ranged from $682 to $87,629. For hearts, the range was from $390 to $60,000. These charges included transporting organs from place to place, surgeon's fees, lab tests, hospital costs, and charges by the agency that coordinated the transplant.

Transplantation consumes many health care dollars. Each year, more than 400 babies are born with biliary atresia, a disease in the liver. A liver transplant is needed to prevent death in early childhood. The total cost of these transplants amounts to $80 million, and the cost of medication for these patients would be $2 million each year thereafter. Another 5,000 older people need liver transplants each year. More than 15,000 can use a heart transplant. That amounts to more than $4 billion a year to serve 20,000 people.

In transplants, as in other types of health care, some people argue that is unfair if inability to pay deprives people of treatment. However, others contend that health care is a commodity that can be bought and sold. Not everyone can afford the same things, whether it is housing, cars, or clothing. Proponents of this view say that a lack of money for costly health care procedures is unfortunate but not unfair.[1]

Those who disagree say that health care is more important than homes, cars, or clothing. They believe all citizens are entitled to a minimum amount of health care, which now includes intensive care for cardiac disease. They say transplants should be part of this minimum level of benefits. Transplants may be less expensive in the long run than maintaining people on life-support systems. As of 1990, the first year of care for a kidney transplant patient costs about $80,000, and about $7,000 a year thereafter for drug treatment to prevent rejection. This compares to about $33,000 a year for kidney dialysis treatments. Also, after a transplant, many people resume productive lives as workers and taxpayers.

WHO WILL BE CHOSEN?

People have suggested various systems for allocating organs. One is a free-market approach, selling organs to those who can afford to pay. Another is a case-by-case assessment of patients' social value, in terms of their roles and contributions. A related method would consider a person's status or entitlement, for instance giving preference to veterans. A lottery system could be used, or organs could be distributed strictly on the basis of medical need.[2]

Dr. Carl Greiner, psychiatric consultant to a transplant center in Omaha, Nebraska, says that these choices center around questions of justice, and he lists five rival theories of justice:

- Provide for those in greatest need.
- Provide for those with the greatest chance of success.
- Provide for those who have made the greatest contribution.
- Provide for those with the ability to pay.
- Provide by lottery.[3]

Greiner says that whenever we decide who will receive an organ, we must be able to give a rational explanation and state which principles of justice are involved.[4] He contends that the current system for allocating organs often focuses on the first two concerns, choosing patients who have the greatest need and rejecting those with less than a 20 percent chance of survival.

Greiner says that decisions about who is to receive an organ should not be made solely by physicians. All Americans should understand the issues and discuss them. The public should join with health care professionals to set policies regarding organ transplant technology.[5]

In response to various concerns, Congress passed H.R.-2659 (S-1657) in 1994. It requires the Department of Health and Human Services to develop regulations, rather than guidelines, governing organ transplants. This bill asks for a single list of potential organ recipients for each regional organ-provider organization, rather than different lists generated at each center. Organs would be allocated based on strict medical criteria, and citizens and resident aliens would receive absolute priority over foreigners. (As of 1994, 10 percent of all available organs were allocated for foreign nationals.) Congress also asked that community members and consumer groups be included in transplant center boards.

FINDING MORE DONORS

A critical need for donors persists. The Uniform Anatomical Gift Act of 1968 has been adopted by every state and the District of Columbia. People can sign up as organ donors when they renew their driver's license or in other simple ways. Donor cards allow organs to be taken at the time of death without permission from relatives.

But the supply of organs and tissues for transplantation has not increased markedly. Fewer than 20 percent of all Americans have signed donor cards, and cards may not be located at the time of death. Also, some hospitals refuse to take organs unless the family gives permission, which must be secured during a traumatic time. In 1986, Congress said that hospitals receiving Medicare or Medicaid funding must ask bereaved families to consider organ donation. New York and several other states allow coroners to take a dead person's corneas if they are not aware of a clear objection.

Perhaps more people would donate organs if they were paid? The 1984 National Organ Transplantation Act forbids buying or selling organs. Opponents of this policy believe that since hospitals and others benefit financially from transplant operations, so should the donors or their families. Money might motivate more people to donate organs, just as it motivates some people to become surrogate mothers. Yet there is a potential for criminal networks that smuggle organs and sell organs to the highest bidders.

Law professor Linda Fentiman has proposed a new attitude toward organ donation—viewing donation not as an act of altruism but as a community obligation. The government could implement a system that presumes consent on the part of all mentally competent people over age eighteen. People could state an objection to donation when renewing their driver's license, filing an income tax return, or applying for welfare. Several European nations, New Zealand, Tunisia, and Singapore have instituted systems of presumed consent.

Donors or their survivors could be compensated with cash, vouchers for college tuition, payment of burial expenses, or a tax-deductible gift to a favorite charity.[6] Payment might encourage more poor people than wealthy to donate organs. However, this happens in other areas of life when people need money.

FETAL TISSUE TRANSPLANTS

During President Ronald Reagan's administration, a ban on federal funding for fetal research went into effect. Reagan and others who opposed abortion thought that such research might encourage abortions. After President Bill Clinton lifted the ban in 1993, more fetal tissue became available for research. Scientists have experimented with fetal tissues in transplant therapy and are using them to study ways to genetically engineer cell growth from fetal tissue.

Fetal tissue transplants have aided victims of Parkinson's disease. In one case, after fetal cells were implanted into the brain of a fifty-three-year-old man with Parkinson's, they grew and made the right connections. Says Dr. Curt Freed, "We have people who now can walk and talk and hold a job who couldn't do that before."[7]

Fetal pancreas tissue has been injected into diabetics, who cannot make their own insulin. Such transplants may reduce the need for medication and prevent complications of diabetes, such as blindness, high blood pressure, and nerve damage.

But, as with organs, there is more demand than the supply can meet. During the 1990s, scientists were able to use only a small percentage of embryos and fetuses for transplantation. Many are contaminated with bacteria or contain chromosomal abnormalities that could lead to cancer in recipients.[8]

Many people still feel that fetal tissue should not be collected. Others are concerned about who will collect such tissues and under what circumstances, as well as what safety standards will aim to ensure that fetal tissue (and other organs) are free of viruses and bacteria. They also wonder if clinics might change the way they perform abortions in order to obtain fetuses that are more intact, making them more usable for research and transplants.[9]

THORNY DILEMMAS

Some recurring transplant cases show the complex issues involved. Consider the case of anencephalic babies, born without the cerebral portion of the brain, which is used for thinking, reasoning, self-awareness, and communication. They are usually stillborn or die within weeks. The brain stem is present, allowing hearts and lungs to function, and sometimes, the hearts or other organs can be transplanted to help another child. If the baby is stillborn and is not resuscitated, the organs might deteriorate, making them unsuitable for transplantation. But is it right to resuscitate or perform other possibly painful procedures on a baby that is born dying? Is the baby brain-dead? What should the family and doctors do in view of the fact that infant organ donors are rare?

Other debates rage over whether some organ recipients are less worthy than others. Should transplants be denied to people whose health problems are viewed as self-inflicted—for example, those whose liver disease came after years of alcohol or drug abuse? This debate arose again in June 1995 when baseball legend

Mickey Mantle was admitted to a hospital near death because of liver disease and a cancerous liver tumor. Mantle had publicly admitted to years of heavy drinking. When he received his transplant within forty-eight hours after being placed on the waiting list, critics wondered if he had been shown special consideration or if doctors had exaggerated the severity of his condition. When Mantle died in August, critics complained that doctors had used a valuable organ on someone whose cancer had spread beyond his liver, a condition that keeps patients from receiving a transplant.

Doctors claimed that Mantle's case had been treated like any other and that they had performed the necessary tests before surgery and found no evidence that his cancer had spread. They pointed out that the average waiting time for critically ill patients like Mantle in the Dallas, Texas, area is 3.3 days. The medical team offered to share Mantle's medical records with an objective panel of experts.

Should different standards apply to transplant patients? At present, patients with a history of drug or alcohol abuse are asked to seek treatment and to abstain from using these substances to avoid a relapse. Not all comply. But other patients are not denied treatment based on why they need it—for example, accident victims who did not wear seatbelts, or obese people who experience heart attacks.

What about convicted criminals—should they receive transplants? Health care is generally funded by the prison system with tax dollars. This means that convicted murderers, to take an extreme case, might receive a transplant at public expense while low-income working people bear the cost alone. Ethicist Jeffrey Paul contends that the gravity of a crime should determine whether an inmate is eligible for publicly funded care. A person who commits certain crimes may forfeit certain rights and privileges.[10] For example, convicted felons may not vote, join the armed forces, or practice law.

Should certain people receive more than one transplant while others on the list are awaiting their first? This may occur when a person rejects one transplant and is given medical priority for a second.

A related dilemma is whether one patient should be given more than one organ at a time. Paul T. Menzel, a professor of philosophy at Pacific Lutheran University in Tacoma, Washington, cites the case of Laura Davies. At age five, Laura, who had been born without functioning intestines, received small and large intestines, a liver, stomach, pancreas, and two kidneys. It was thought that she had a fifty-fifty chance to survive, but she lived only eight weeks longer and died in November 1993. Menzel expresses compassion for the family's situation but questions the wisdom of this kind of procedure.

Transplant programs have said that a person who needs more than one organ has a more urgent medical condition than those who need one. But Menzel says, "Certainly I am as close to death's door if 'just' my heart fails as I am if my heart and liver both fail." He adds,

> We continually strive to expand the organ pool. Why? To save more lives, obviously. If with that expanded supply, we wind up saving no more people than before because we use up enough of our organ bank on multiple organ recipients, what has been the point of our supply expansion efforts? . . . How can transplant centers justify ultimately letting two or more persons somewhere down the queue likely die because they have drawn so much out of the organ bank to save one?[11]

Another issue is whether transplants should go to people in the donor's country or community when there is more than one suitable recipient, both equally needy. It has been suggested that donated organs be kept in the community if possible, not sent to large, wealthy regional transplant centers. Many Americans think preference should be given to U.S. citizens and residents, since the organs come from Americans and organizations that handle the transplants use public funds. Says Jeffrey M. Protass, "Sending organs overseas or transplanting them into [foreigners who come seeking transplants] is not sharing America's bounty with others but diverting its scarcity."[12]

However, Olga Jonasson points out that scientific advances such as transplantation are built upon work done in various countries. She says, "American medicine has a strong tradition and long history of generously sharing its medical technology and therapies. . . . Transplantation is unavailable in developing countries and in most of the impoverished areas of the world."[13]

Artificial organs may ease organ scarcities, but cost remains a factor. It costs more than $100,000 per patient to surgically implant an artificial heart.[14] The costs and benefits, as well as various ethical concerns, will continue to spark debates about transplants and other life-prolonging technologies.

SEVEN

Prolonging Life

A premature baby, weighing 1½ pounds, survives birth. None of its organ systems can function without artificial help—the lungs cannot take in air needed to oxygenate the blood, the heart cannot pump blood throughout the body, the immature nervous system cannot regulate blood pressure or sustain breathing or heart function. The brain is not fully developed, and excess fluid has killed brain cells. Should every effort be made to save this baby?

The process of dying has changed greatly during the twentieth century. Up until 1950, half of all Americans still died at home. Today, about 80 percent die in hospitals or nursing homes, cared for by strangers. Chronic diseases have replaced infections and acute illnesses as the leading causes of death. People with no cortical—higher brain—function can be kept alive for weeks, even years, with respirators, surgery, drugs, and tube-feedings.

In light of this, new legal definitions of death have replaced older ones based on the lack of a heartbeat or breathing or nonresponsiveness to stimuli. Newer definitions revolve around whether the cortex of the brain is functioning. Ethicists who support this idea say that cortical functioning distinguishes humans from lower animals, encompassing the capacity for self-awareness, memory, emotions, and communication.[1]

Ethical dilemmas abound in this area of medicine. Medical tradition dating back to the Hippocratic oath says that doctors must never harm patients. But often, it is unclear what will do the most harm—keeping someone alive or allowing that person to die. It may be hard to determine whether it is life or death that is being prolonged. In addition, fears of malpractice suits may prompt caregivers to take measures they consider futile.

The cost of life-prolonging treatment adds complications we may wish not to acknowledge. Some patients are indigent, so public funds pay their health care bills. Huge bills may be passed on to a family if the patient dies. Many public hospitals are in debt and in danger of closing. Insurance companies finance increasing costs by raising rates. Hospitals spread the cost of treating the poor among their paying patients, too.

Two major goals of medical treatment are to promote life and to alleviate suffering. Today's powerful treatments may keep people alive but not relieve suffering. They may even increase it. In response to this concern, the President's Commission on Biomedical Ethical Issues said, "The attempt to postpone death should at times yield to other, more important goals of patients."[2]

Hospitals seek to resolve these dilemmas through ethics committees, case-by-case analyses, and policies regarding when to implement heroic measures. Some hospitals divide patients into categories that determine how much care is appropriate: for those with an excellent or good chance of recovery, they may initiate all-out efforts. For the hopelessly ill who will not recover, care focuses on making people comfortable. Yet the rights of various parties may conflict, and individual cases are murky.

TREATMENT BEFORE BIRTH

Sometimes, life-threatening problems develop inside the uterus. Problems that are not beyond help may be treated with vitamins, drugs, blood transfusions, or surgery. As more conditions are being diagnosed before birth and new treatments are developed, decisions about whether to treat the unborn have become more commonplace.

In performing surgery on a fetus, doctors seldom know how far the damage has progressed, so the outcome is in doubt. A fetus may be saved but be born later with handicaps, some requiring lifelong institutionalization. Also, most such treatments are experimental and the fetus has no way to consent.

Two conditions that have been surgically treated in the uterus are obstructions of the urinary tract and hydrocephalus—excess fluid around the brain. Some surgery is successful, but in many cases where hydrocephalus has been treated in the uterus, the babies were born severely handicapped. The mother of a four-year-old son who survived this surgery is bitter that he is severely mentally retarded, bedridden, and often in pain. However, another family has a healthy five-year-old who also had the surgery. Ethicist B. D. Colen asks, "If we have the ability to provide unquestionably beneficial fetal therapy, are we obligated to provide it? If we are, how do we balance the conflicting rights of the two patients in each case, the mother and the fetus?"[3]

The potential to perform surgery on a fetus removed from the uterus creates other dilemmas. If the fetus should take air into its lungs, it could not return to the fluid environment of the uterus afterwards. If fetuses become surgical patients, does this mean they should have a legal status and the rights of any citizen? The answer would affect the ongoing debate over abortion.

The use of modern fertility drugs may cause multiple pregnancies, sometimes six embryos or more. Some embryos can be destroyed in the uterus, giving others a better chance to develop.

Doctors selectively abort embryos whose positions in the uterus give them the least chance of survival. People who have chosen this procedure say they feared that all the embryos might die if left to develop. Other parents let nature take its course. In many cases, their babies were stillborn or premature and handicapped. But the parents still believe it is immoral to end life before birth.

SAVING NEWBORNS AT RISK

Grave ethical concerns surround the use of heroic treatment to save newborns who would otherwise die. In America, more than 300,000 infants are born each year with physical and/or mental abnormalities. Such births occur in all ethnic, racial, and economic groups, affecting millions of families around the world.[4]

About 5 percent of all babies need specialized care because of genetic disorders or, more often, prematurity. Electronic monitors, mechanical ventilators, special intravenous fluids, and advanced surgical techniques sustain such infants. In 1960, 70 percent of all infants who weighed less than 3 pounds, 5 ounces died; today about 30 percent do. About 85 percent of the babies in intensive care units survive.

Some babies die at birth unless they are resuscitated. A number of doctors admit that, in rare cases, they have decided to let severely abnormal infants die in the delivery room, often furtively.

When babies are born ten or more weeks early or with serious defects, a decision must be made as to whether intensive care will prolong the dying process or result in life—and what the quality of that life will be. Yet many people cannot imagine *not* giving treatment when a baby is born alive. Once treatment has begun, then people must decide if it is ever appropriate to stop.

In 1975, a group of pediatricians convened a panel of twenty people from medicine, nursing, law, sociology, psychology, ethics, social work, economics, and anthropology to analyze five difficult cases. All agreed that, under certain conditions, it is ethical not to resuscitate and also to withdraw life support from infants who clearly had a poor prognosis. Seventeen said there were cases in which it would be all right to kill a premature infant that was slowly dying. One was uncertain; the other two disagreed.[5]

Cases of spina bifida (myelomeningocele) show the dilemmas that can arise when there are serious birth defects. The spinal cord does not develop properly, and part of the cord has little or no insulating covering, leaving an exposed area that is prone to infection. Once, 80 percent of all babies with spina bifida died, but today 90 percent survive. Surgeons can close the spinal opening and drain the fluid from the brain, shunting it to the abdomen or another place where it can be absorbed.

But, is this procedure truly ethical? Does it benefit the child? Later, these children may face many problems. At least 40 percent are mentally retarded. About half are paralyzed from the waist down and lack bowel or bladder control. Recurring swelling of the brain tissue may require additional shunts, which must be replaced periodically. Spinal curvatures, dislocated hips, humping of the back, and kidney disease are also common.

In the 1970s, Dr. John Lorber, the British surgeon who developed the shunt technique, studied the outcome for 848 infants who were treated between 1959 and 1968. Fifty percent did not survive, despite surgery and advanced treatment. Only 1.4 percent of the survivors had no handicaps. Of the rest, more than 80 percent had severe physical handicaps, and about half were mentally retarded. About 17 percent had moderate handicaps, such as a lack of bladder control. Many had had several operations, even a dozen or more. Lorber said,

> These babies now live with distressing physical or mental handicaps or both, often for many years, without hope of ever having an independent existence compatible with human dignity. . . . The problems we created

were greater than those we solved. Treating all babies without selection resulted in much more suffering for large numbers.[6]

COSTS AND BENEFITS OF SAVING INFANTS

Although people may hate to consider economics when a life is at stake, the subject of cost comes up when high-tech care is used, especially when outcomes are doubtful. During the early 1980s, one study found that the average cost for intensive care of babies weighing under 1.64 pounds was more than $100,000. The cost of producing one survivor was more than $200,000. Intensive care for low birth-weight infants is extremely costly, produces few survivors, and even fewer healthy ones, say experts.[7]

This unpleasant reality was noted by Canadian researchers, who said, "By every measure of economic evaluation, it was economically more favorable to provide intensive care for the relatively heavier infants [weighing 2.19 to 3.28 pounds at birth] than for those weighing [1.1 to 2.185 pounds]."[8] Therefore, some experts suggest that infants below a certain weight not be placed on mechanical ventilators and receive only fluids, warmth, and care in the special nursery, along with oxygen through a plastic hood.

However, there are pitfalls to setting an arbitrary cut-off point, below which extensive care will be denied. Individual babies differ greatly in their prenatal history, developmental age, and overall makeup. Some tiny infants (including one born in 1979 who weighed 15 ounces) grow and develop appropriately.

WHO DECIDES?

In America, parents, not the state, generally make decisions about themselves and their children. At the same time, laws protect children from potentially harmful parental decisions or actions. In 1982, in Bloomington, Indiana, parents, with the approval of a doctor, refused heroic treatment to save a newborn with serious abnormalities. Courts had usually authorized doctors to save a child against parental wishes, but this time, the court let the parents choose to withhold life-saving treatment. The infant, referred to in the media as Baby Doe, died six days after birth.

In the wake of this conflict, the Reagan administration issued a "Notice to Health Care Providers" from the Office of Civil Rights, which became known as the "Baby Doe rules." It informed hospitals that federal law barred them from denying any treatment to handicapped patients that would normally be given to the nonhandicapped. Specifically, they could not withhold from a handicapped infant "nutritional sustenance or medical or surgical treatment required to correct a life-threatening condition if: (1) the withholding is based on the fact that the infant is handicapped and (2) the handicap does not render the treatment or nutritional sustenance medically contraindicated."[9]

In March 1983, the Department of Health and Human Services expanded the Baby Doe rules. All hospitals receiving federal funds were required to post obvious warnings in delivery rooms, maternity wards, pediatric units, and nurseries that read: "Discriminatory failure to feed and care for handicapped infants in this facility is prohibited by federal law." A hotline number was listed so that anyone could report infractions.

Critics called this a "snitch rule" and invasion into family decisions that could cause much suffering. Despite good intentions, it might not be compassionate. The chief justice of the Indiana Supreme Court, which had refused to intervene on behalf of Baby Doe, said, "There's no need for any legislation. . . . We can't pass a law saying doctors have to save every child that's born."[10]

A group that included the American Academy of Pediatrics challenged the Baby Doe rules, which were struck down by a federal district court in April 1983. Revised rules issued early in 1984 stated that treatment need not include "impossible or futile acts of therapy." The revised regulations allowed hospitals to create committees to advise doctors on these cases. Many hospitals already had ethics committees to safeguard patients' rights, especially those of children or incompetent people. The committees may include people from medicine, the clergy, law, ethics, social work, and the disabled. Some hospitals have physiological and mental criteria to help committees decide who should receive heroic treatment.

Since 1982, federal investigators have dealt with hundreds of alleged violations of the Baby Doe rules. Health-care givers often fear that if a baby dies for lack of heroic treatment, the doctor, parents, and hospital may be sued for child abuse, neglect, or even homicide. Says Dr. M. Harry Jennison, former executive director of the American Academy of Pediatrics, "Regrettably, the solutions sometimes rendered [in court] have been founded on the premise that *all* life, no matter how compromised and miserable—must be maintained if that is technically possible."[11] Many doctors believe that parents should make the decisions after consulting with doctors, relatives, and clergymen. Those who have witnessed these situations say that such decisions are not made lightly.

Pediatrician William Silverman faults doctors who fail to consider the social and family context in these cases, saying, "When parents with marginal financial and emotional resources are overwhelmed by the survival of a sickly or malformed neonate [newborn], the situation becomes a prescription for disaster."[12] Only about half of the seriously handicapped children who need homes are adopted, usually those with physical handicaps.

Jeffrey Lyon worries that a court focuses only on whether it is medically possible to extend life: "It presupposes that longer life is universally preferable to death, enshrining existence as a kind of religion. And it rests on the assumption that because it is morally offensive to proclaim one person's life more or less meaningful than another's, one may never attempt to render judgment on any infant's quality of life."[13] Lyon asks,

> Should we as a society insist on preserving the lives of the most severely handicapped of these children—those who in former times would have died—only to bestow on them a substandard existence of incapacity, banishment, and pain? And why should a couple's innocent desire for children condemn them to a lifetime with a child who bankrupts them emotionally and financially and perhaps destroys their marriage? Should the act of reproduction be such an awesome roll of the dice?[14]

DETERMINING THE PATIENT'S BEST INTERESTS

Doctors looking at the same patient, whether infant or adult, may disagree about the risks, future pain and suffering, or prognosis. People also disagree about what is an acceptable quality of life. Children with Down syndrome, for instance, vary greatly in terms of physical and mental functioning. Many parents love and enjoy these children, and some families seek to adopt them. A number of ethicists agree that mental retardation alone is not a reason to withhold life-saving treatment. They consider the severity of physical problems and degree of suffering a child might endure.

Some ethicists say that we should ask whether we ourselves would want to live under certain circumstances: How much suffering and deprivation are involved? Jeffrey Lyon decries the tendency to discuss newborns "in a strangely disembodied way, as if they were subordinate to the larger issue." He says,

> At times, unreality takes over and disabilities of the most grievous kind are sanitized so that they sound less devas-

tating than they really are. We are told that a Baby Ashley will be capable of smiling if caressed on the cheek. We are told that a Baby Jane Doe may not be completely bedridden and may at least be vaguely aware of her surroundings. The implication is that minimal lives do not have to be bad and can even be enjoyable and fulfilling. But to test the nobility of these sentiments we have only to reflect on whether we would wish to experience such a life. Chances are, most of us would not. Why then do we ask the congenitally impaired to endure more suffering, pain, and endless boredom than we would want for ourselves?[15]

Lyon believes that "although we may not be able to describe the precise point at which the level of handicap becomes too dismal, most of us have an intuitive knowledge of where that point is."[16] After analyzing hundreds of cases and talking with families, Lyon found that people based their decisions on the intensity of a child's suffering, his or her potential for forming relationships, and the ability of the family to care for the child.

Advocates of saving all infants raise "slippery slope" arguments. They worry that declaring certain babies "unfit to live" implies a lack of respect for people with handicaps. In response, some ethicists say that while life is always sacred, a certain kind of life may be unbearable. Lyon sees a difference between saying a life is not worthy to be lived and that some lives are not worthwhile to be lived—"that they are so ridden with pain, distress, and ennui that they may be of negative value to their owner."[17]

Most experts support case-by-case analyses, saying that no single set of guidelines will apply to all. These painful decisions are fraught with emotional, social, and economic implications.

In some cases, severely injured people regain consciousness and choose to live. When twenty-four-year-old Armando Dimas arrived at a Houston emergency room, X rays showed that a bullet was lodged high in his spinal cord too near the brain to be removed. He would be paralyzed from the jaw down, unable to breathe, doctors explained to the family. But the family insisted Dimas would recover and that such a large, modern hospital could help him walk and breathe again. They also insisted that he not be told the grim prognosis, although doctors thought Dimas had the right to help decide his own fate.

When they finally did inform him, he blinked a response that indicated he wanted to live. Dimas had no health insurance. His family, Mexican immigrants seeking legal status, was destitute although very hardworking. The hospital had serious financial problems and was $4 million in debt at the time. Armando Dimas received inpatient care for four and a half years at a cost of $727,008.71 before the hospital was able to place him in an extended care facility with an excellent reputation. Eventually, the family learned how to care for him at home. He learned to sit in a custom-made wheelchair, to speak, and to eat. Of his life, Dimas says, "I see my family. I go outside a lot. In a lot of ways, things are good. . . . This is the way it is. That's all."[18]

EIGHT
The Right to Refuse Treatment

IN APRIL 1975, TWENTY-ONE-YEAR-OLD KAREN QUINLAN went into a coma after ingesting alcohol and drugs. She did not meet the legal criteria for death, since there was electrical activity in the brain, but Quinlan could not see, talk, think, or feel. She was attached to a respirator for a year, until her parents received permission from the New Jersey Supreme Court to remove it. The court ruled that, in certain cases, the right to privacy and the privilege of choosing death take precedence over the duty of the state to preserve life. The court also used a "substitute judgment test," saying that the family must try to imagine what Karen would want. In March 1976, the respirator was turned off, but Quinlan did not die. She received medication, feedings, and nursing care in the years that followed. Her life finally ceased in 1985.

More than seventeen states permit termination of life support in certain cases. In Quinlan's case, tube feedings and intravenous infusions kept her biologically alive. Comparing these procedures to the use of artificial respirators, courts have allowed family and doctors to terminate them, too. In 1991, the U.S. Supreme Court permitted this to be done in *Cruzan v. Director, Missouri Department of Health*.[1] In 1985, at age twenty-six, Nancy Cruzan had an auto accident that left her in a persistent vegetative state. A few years later, her parents asked that her feeding tube be removed. It had been inserted shortly after the accident when doctors hoped she might recover. Some of Cruzan's nurses disagreed with the decision and said that Cruzan had moments of awareness and responsiveness.

The matter of terminating life support has also been debated from religious perspectives. In 1957, Pope Pius XII said that physicians have a duty to use ordinary means to heal patients but do not have to provide treatments that "cannot be obtained or used without excessive expense, pain, or other inconvenience, or which, if used, would not offer a reasonable hope of benefit."[2] Catholic, Protestant, Jewish, Hindu, Buddhist, and Moslem ethicists have said there is no moral duty to preserve life in *all* terminal cases.[3]

The President's Commission for the Study of Ethical Problems in Medicine and Biomedical and Behavioral Research suggested several guidelines for analyzing these situations:

- Respect the choices of individuals who are competent (in other words, consider a patient's autonomy).
- Provide mechanisms and guidelines for decision-making when patients are unable to choose on their own.
- Maintain a presumption in favor of sustaining life.
- Improve medical options available to dying patients.
- Give respectful, responsive, and supportive care to patients for whom no further medical therapies are available or elected (a consideration of beneficence to the patient).
- Encourage health care institutions to take responsibility for ensuring that adequate procedures for decision-making are available for all patients (a guideline that highlights matters of justice).[4]

Jeffrey Lyon offers this opinion:

No worthy purpose is served by the strapping of an individual to a set of exotic machines if the result is merely to keep insensate flesh alive. . . . By the same token, keeping alive by heroic means a fully conscious patient whose disease is hopeless and who is in extreme pain is not only senseless but cruel. For these reasons, the law permits a competent adult to refuse treatment if he or she so desires.[5]

MAY YOUNG PEOPLE REFUSE TREATMENT?

In October 1994, teenage Billy Best ran away from home. Best had been receiving chemotherapy and radiation treatments for Hodgkin's disease, a cancer of the lymph glands, and he wanted to avoid further treatment. In a letter to his parents, he wrote, "I could not stand going to the hospital every week. I feel like the medicine is killing me instead of helping me."[6] He later called his parents to tell them he was all right and was living somewhere in Texas.

Early in 1995, Best came home but did not resume treatment. His cancer appeared to be in remission, which doctors attributed to his previous drug therapy, but later, he died.

Courts usually allow mentally competent adults to refuse treatment, but what about minors? Since the 1930s, U.S. courts have allowed minors, usually those over age fourteen, to give informed consent regarding health services even if their parents disagree. A doctor must determine that the teenager understands the nature of his or her condition, the treatment being offered, and the benefits, risks, and alternatives.

Doctors using this approach say that they still try to persuade young people to receive treatment, then help them to get through it. They may spend a great deal of time talking with parents and teens, as well as recommending support groups and giving teens some choices about aspects of their treatment.

Fifteen-year-old Benito Agrelo of Florida also decided to stop medical treatment. Agrelo had undergone two liver transplants and found the side effects of the antirejection medication unbearable. When he stopped taking the drug, the state health department ordered that he be removed from his parents' home and placed in a Miami hospital. A circuit court judge ruled that Agrelo had the right to stop treatment. He died on August 20, 1994, at his home.

In a case that dealt with cultural issues as well, a fifteen-year-old Californian, Lee Lor, left home to avoid cancer treatments. Days earlier, police acting under a court order obtained by the department of social services had tried to take her forcibly to a hospital. They also considered placing her in a foster home so that her family could not keep her away from treatment.

The Lor family was part of a community of Hmong refugees from a southeast Asian mountain region where people rely on herbs and other ancient medical treatments and spiritual healing. The community thought Lee Lor should not have to accept Western medicine. Without treatment, doctors said she had only a 10 percent chance of surviving, while treatment would raise her chances to 80 percent. The debate over Lee Lor's fate continued in 1995.[7]

Suppose an unborn child could die unless a blood transfusion is given, but the parent's religion forbids it? Jehovah's Witnesses believe the Bible forbids blood transfusions. Yet courts have required parents to submit to treatment in order to safeguard a fetus. And though adults may refuse treatment for themselves on religious grounds, courts have required parents to obtain treatment for their minor children.

APPROPRIATE CARE FOR THE ELDERLY

Many ethical concerns surround health care for the elderly, who may differ greatly in their degree of wellness and functioning. People ask whether it is proper to use life-support systems or surgery on senile elderly people, for example, or those for whom death seems imminent. A practical concern is the cost of heroic care. B. D. Colen says, "The often used term 'extraordinary means' encompasses expenses that would create an 'extraordinary' burden to a patient or a patient's family."[8]

One doctor has a patient in his nineties who has had several heart attacks and a series of strokes. The man, totally helpless, receives oxygen through plastic tubes inserted in his nostrils; another tube drains urine from his bladder. Some of his many drugs cause unpleasant side-effects. His doctor fears that heroic measures will continue, while the man's family agonizes over him and worries about the bills. Doctors say they have no good answers when family members ask why such patients cannot die in peace.

There is mounting concern about meeting the needs of older people and delivering care that reflects respect and compassion. People worry that elderly people may feel pressured or so guilty that they refuse care they really want. Economic pressures may prompt state agencies to limit care for the elderly or move them into cheaper facilities where care is less skilled.

Daniel Callahan, director of the Hastings Center, a bioethical think-tank, thinks that society must define more clearly what duties the young owe the old, and vice versa. In *Setting Limits: Medical Goals in an Aging Society*, Callahan says that the focus of medicine for elderly people should be on improving the quality of life rather than just extending it. He bemoans the lack of humane, adequately funded long-term care facilities as well as a lack of resources that would help families care well for elderly members.[9] Others agree, saying, "The remarkable ability of medicine to extend life has not been matched by a similar capacity to insure a high level of health and individual flourishing."[10] Diseases of older people, such as Alzheimer's, that require long-term, expensive care make these questions all the more compelling.

ASSISTED SUICIDE

Allowing someone to die by removing or not using heroic treatment is different from actively helping someone to die, something most health-care givers refuse to do. Euthanasia—choosing to die—can be direct or indirect, done by an individual alone or with help. For example, Elizabeth Bouvia, a cerebral palsy victim paralyzed from the neck down, asked a hospital to help her starve to death while keeping her comfortable. The hospital refused.

Those who find euthanasia acceptable may give a higher value to well-being or the reduction of suffering than being alive in itself. Humanistic and personalistic ethical viewpoints hold that it is harder to justify letting someone die slowly in pain than to end that suffering through death. Others say that these matters are for God, not humans, to decide.

Advocates of legalizing doctor-assisted suicide say it would help the terminally ill to die more comfortably. Between 1990 and 1995, Dr. Jack Kevorkian, a retired pathologist in Detroit, helped more than twenty gravely ill people end their lives, usually by administering carbon monoxide. Michigan officials arrested Kevorkian several times, and in 1992, the state legislature enacted a bill to ban suicide assistance. A state commission studied the issue but did not come up with definitive suggestions for the legislature. Kevorkian has pledged to continue helping those who ask to die, despite a new bill proposed in 1994 that would make assisting in a suicide a felony punishable by up to four years in prison.

In 1994, Oregon became the first state to allow terminally ill persons to obtain prescriptions for lethal drugs that would help them die. The Death With Dignity Act included such safeguards as requiring that two doctors determine the person had less than six months to live and had rejected all other alternatives. Patients must make three requests for the prescription, the third in writing. They are expected to take the drug on their own.

A federal district court in Washington State also said that as long as terminally ill patients are competent, they may obtain help from a consenting physician to kill themselves. The group called Compassion in Dying had asked the court to rule on this matter.

Roman Catholic clergymen have protested these decisions. Archbishop William J. Levada called the Oregon act "murder in the name of mercy" and told Catholics to reject it.[11] Human Life International, an active pro-life group, also protested the act. The Oregon Medical Association did not voice a position.

Robert A. Burt, a law professor at Yale University, worries that "the poor, elderly, unassertive, clinically depressed, members of disfavored minorities or some combination of these—would be especially vulnerable to subtle or not so subtle prompting to choose a quick, easy (and inexpensive) exit."[12] Burk says that more should be done to help the terminally ill, such as hospice and home care and painkillers for their individual needs. The terminally ill are often abandoned when they need support and comfort, says Burt.

LIVING WILLS

Many people question the idea of prolonging life at any cost. The nonprofit organization Choice in Dying received more than 3,000 calls a day during the week after former First Lady Jacqueline Kennedy Onassis died. Onassis had declined heroic care for terminal cancer and chose to die at home amid family and friends.[13]

Advance directives, such as living wills and medical powers of attorney, are legal documents that describe the care a person would want if incapacitated. They emerged during the "death with dignity" movement of the 1960s, as people discussed the place of death in the life cycle. The documents cover the use of cardiopulmonary resuscitation (CPR), mechanical breathing, major surgery, blood transfusions, artificial nutrition, and extended care.

One will, from the Euthanasia Educational Council in New York City, reads: "If the situation should arise in which there is no reasonable expectation of my recovery from physical or mental disability, I request that I be allowed to die and not be kept alive by artificial means or 'heroic measures.'" This document was first published in 1969. By 1975, more than 750,000 copies were in print, and by end of 1977, during intense media coverage of the Quinlan case, this figure had doubled.

In 1991, Congress passed a law that requires hospitals and nursing homes receiving federal funds to inform patients that they may sign such directives and may also refuse certain treatments.

Having a living will may not guarantee it will be honored. Sometimes, relatives try to overrule the advance instructions of patients who have asked to be disconnected from life support if they are judged to be in an irreversible coma. Hospitals also have not honored all such requests. In one case, after a hospital disregarded the living will of a seventy-year-old woman with lung cancer, a court ruled that her rights were not lost when she became comatose and that the living will constituted informed consent.

Even when living wills exist, some issues may remain: What is a reasonable expectation of recovery? What extent of physical or mental disability would be unacceptable to the person? What are the family's motives if and when they disagree with the patient's directives? Moral theologian John Connery, professor at Loyola University, said, "Most people are in favor of making quality-of-life decisions, but we have no norms, no way to draw lines in regard to quality of life. What quality of life is above the standard, and what quality of life is below?"[14]

WHEN DOCTORS AND FAMILIES DISAGREE

In Virginia, a legal debate centered around an infant known as Baby K. Doctors at Fairfax County Hospital agreed that Baby K, born without much of her brain, would never see, hear, feel, think, have memories, or be conscious. She had reflexes, functions that are handled in the brain stem. The mother insisted that she be kept alive, and a federal appeals court ordered the hospital to aggressively help Baby K when she had severe breathing problems, a regular occurrence. Feeding was done through tubes.

The court based its decision on the "anti-dumping law," passed to protect uninsured people a hospital might wish to transfer in order to save money, and on the 1990 Americans with Disabilities Act. The act bans discrimination based on physical condition and states that the disabled must receive the same treatment that would be given to someone without a disability. Under the federal Child Abuse Act, doctors must also treat seriously damaged or premature infants despite a poor prognosis and regardless of quality of life.

The hospital appealed the court verdict and said that instead of prolonging Baby K's life, treatment was prolonging her death. "Without constant heroic support, Baby K will die of natural causes," said one doctor.[15] He noted that if society is unwilling to withhold care in a case as bleak as this, then "we can forget about reducing health care costs." By the summer of 1994, the cost for twenty-month-old Baby K had reached $250,000, paid by insurance. The baby was moved to a nursing home where Medicaid, the public health insurance fund, would pay $30,000 a year. The court said that Congress must change the laws if it wishes to allow hospitals to deny treatment in hopeless cases.

When doctors and family members agree, such cases are handled more easily. But conflicts arise when, after discussing the case, family members or the doctor and the family cannot reach an agreement. Should doctors be required to prolong the life of a patient when they believe it is futile, but the family wants it?

In 1995, a lawsuit was filed against a doctor at Massachusetts General Hospital in Boston who refused to use extraordinary measures to keep alive a comatose woman with irreversible brain damage. The seventy-one-year-old patient had entered the hospital in 1989 for hip surgery. She suffered from diabetes, heart disease, urinary problems, and Parkinson's disease, and had been treated for cancer and a stroke. Before surgery began, she had several seizures that left her in a coma. An ethics committee at the hospital authorized a "do not resuscitate" order, which was put on her chart.

The patient's daughter said she had suffered great mental anguish because her mother's wishes were not followed and sued the doctor and the hospital. Her attorney argued that the issue is who should make treatment decisions. He claimed that it should not be hospitals or insurance companies, since they may be looking for reasons to end someone's treatment. Experts said this was the first lawsuit of its kind. It was still pending as of 1995.

Some doctors resolve these conflicts by stopping treatment without telling the family or despite their objections. A 1995 survey of American doctors in adult intensive care units showed that 14 percent had withheld or stopped treatment they considered useless without telling family members. More than 80 percent had done so despite objections.[16]

Doctors say that it is not reasonable for patients to ask for every possible treatment, however marginal, then feel betrayed if it is not given. They point out that in many cases, family members are in a state of denial over the condition of loved ones and cannot make sound decisions. John J. Paris, a priest and ethicist at Boston University, said, "We now have the idea that . . . patients' rights mean . . . patients and their surrogates can demand treatment and physicians are obligated to provide it. This is madness. This is not what medicine is about."[17]

A California physician, Dr. Bill Fowkes, says,

I have in my practice an individual who has cost approximately $2.5 million to maintain over the past six years. During the time I have followed her, she has not moved, spoken, or given any indication of consciousness. She is being supported by a tube in her windpipe attached to a respirator, by a tube in her stomach to continuously feed her and [by] around-the-clock nursing care. She has been hospitalized at incredible cost on several occasions. This is not the wish of her providers, who have repeatedly requested that she be allowed to die. The family has insisted that all of this be done, and in our present environment there is no good way to stop this futility. This is not someone who will recover. Are we willing to care for our elders in this manner, when many of our people have no ongoing care?[18]

When deciding such cases, courts tend to order treatment. In the early 1990s, among those whom the courts had ordered kept alive were a Minnesota woman in a chronic vegetative state, a brain-dead teenager in Florida, and Baby K, in Virginia. Such cases may go unresolved for months.

Yet these ethical issues *must* be resolved, not only for the sake of the individuals who are directly affected but for the sake of the larger society. As the year 2000 draws near, one of the most urgent bioethical dilemmas is how to allocate limited health care resources in the most effective and equitable ways.

NINE

Costs and Priorities

- Liver transplants cost about $250,000 for the initial surgery and postoperative care. About two-thirds are successful.[1]
- Kidney dialysis costs about $2.6 billion a year and serves some 60,000 people.[2]
- The largest portion of Medicare funds, about $50 billion, is spent on people who are in the last year of life.[3] This is more than three times what the government spent on medical research in 1994.[4]
- Through public health insurance plans, state and federal governments pay for the health care of some citizens. Should the government be able to tell these people which doctors and health care facilities they may use?
- When funds are limited, should they be used for heroic care to save a few people or to benefit many people, through blood-pressure screenings, childhood immunizations, basic prenatal care?

Ethical dilemmas arise when people make competing claims on limited resources. For example, what happens when the number of patients in an emergency room exceeds the number of caregivers, or when more than one person needs the only empty bed in the intensive care unit? Who receives treatment if two patients go into cardiac arrest and only one team and set of equipment is available?

Other decisions must be made about how to spend health care dollars. When government is providing health care, should the main consideration be to provide care to the most people in the most efficient way or to make sure that individuals receive all the latest treatments and are personally satisfied with their care?

Unlike the dilemmas posed earlier, economic concerns require us to weigh the rights of individuals in relation to other individuals and the rights of individuals in regard to the larger society; complex matters indeed. Individual preferences may conflict with what is best for society as a whole. That is why, in order to guarantee all citizens a minimum level of health care, some nations limit the use of advanced treatments for individuals.

Health care analyst Richard Lamm writes, "We are rapidly sailing into a new and morally painful world of American medicine. The central characteristics of this new world is that we have invented more medicine than we can afford to pay for. Even if we could successfully remove all the inefficiencies from the American medical system, we are still confronted by a new painful reality: Infinite medical needs have run into finite resources."[5]

THE HIGH COST OF HEALTH CARE

As of 1995, America was spending more than $849 billion a year on health care—more than $2 billion a day. Money for health care comes from local, state, and federal government, insurance companies, and individuals. Political leaders, insurance companies, and the public are discussing ways to set health care priorities, contain costs, and use resources more efficiently. After President Bill Clinton took office in 1993, a major debate took place over how to reform the current system. That debate continued into 1995. People were alarmed to hear that Medicare, the insurance system that helps to pay some health care costs for the elderly, might go bankrupt in the near future.

Several factors drive up health care costs in America. One is the idea that life should be saved at all costs, using high-tech diagnostic tools and treatments. The system of third-party payment by insurance companies shields most Americans from the reality of high health care costs. It may also reduce their desire to curb costs since they pay little or none of the bill. But high costs drive up insurance premiums, which affects businesses that insure their employees. Many companies have responded by employing more part-time or freelance employees, whom they need not insure.

Doctors and hospitals have felt free to buy and use new technology and order expensive tests. The U.S. has become a nation of lawsuits. Fearing malpractice suits, doctors may order tests or procedures that they believe are not really necessary. Dr. John W. Scanlon, a pediatrician and neonatologist, says,

> Malpractice costs the public every time they visit a doctor, go to the hospital or pay a health insurance premium. . . . Those extra tests ordered to 'cover all bases,' the reluctance to make a decision that stops heroic but hopeless care, or that detailed description about every possible horrible complication from necessary therapy, can be laid directly to the physician's fear of subsequent malpractice action. Certainly the public needs protection from incompetent, bumbling, thoughtless or just plain stupid medical practice. And make no mistake, lousy care does exist. But it is not prevalent.[6]

Insurance companies and the federally funded Medicare and Medicaid have tried to set priorities. Generally, they have refused to pay for treatments they classified as experimental, outdated, risky, useless, or of questionable value. But in setting limits, insurance companies have been criticized and even sued. In 1994, a court awarded the Fox family $89 million in damages after Mrs. Nelene Fox died of breast cancer. The insurance plan through her health maintenance organization (HMO) had refused to finance a bone marrow transplant, which cost $140,000, that she hoped would save her life.

The transplant was relatively new and the HMO said it was experimental—not yet proven effective or safe—and thus not covered. The treatment involves a complicated surgery and high doses of strong anticancer drugs. About one in four people who have it survive. Nelene Fox did have the transplant eight months later after a community effort raised the needed funds, but she died. Journalists Michael Meyer and Andrew Murr point out that this kind of case shows a major dilemma in American health care—"how to balance demands for high-tech medicine against rising costs."[7]

Richard A. McCormick, a professor of ethics at the University of Notre Dame, says that certain attitudes and values, not always openly acknowledged, strongly influence the health care debate and health care costs. These factors include:

- The denial of mortality: Current health care is organized in a way that rejects the idea of death. McCormick quotes Daniel Callahan of the Hastings Institute: "We have defined our unlimited hopes to transcend our mortality as our needs, and we have created a medical enterprise that engineers the transformation."[8] He cites a 1987 Harris poll in which 71 percent of Americans said that health insurance should pay for any treatment that would save a life, even if it cost a million dollars.[9]

- The eugenic mentality: People have developed a consumer mentality toward reproduction. Parents undergo prenatal screening so that they can choose to discard a child that does not fit their idea of what they want, making parenthood a conditional state.[10]
- Ever-broadening definitions of health and illness. Once, the word *disease* connoted an "identifiable degenerative or inflammatory process that could lead to serious organic illness or death when it continued." Deviations from a supposed norm have become a standard for identifying problems, so that many medical procedures today are done for cosmetic reasons. McCormick says that our society cannot tolerate aging or discomfort.[11]
- The notion that good health care equals efficient rescue medicine. Enthralled by dramatic examples of medical wonders, people may ignore the many preventive factors that are within the patient's control, not a physician's—for example, diet, exercise, and giving up smoking have had a much greater impact on controlling heart disease since the 1970s than bypass surgery or pills for high blood pressure. Emphasizing acute care makes little sense in an aging society, where there is a need for caring, not just curing.[12]
- Absolutization of autonomy: The pendulum has swung away from the idea of doctors' control toward a focus on who has the right to make decisions. Less attention is being paid to whether the choices are good or bad or the features involved.
- Dignity as independence: The idea that having to depend upon others is un-American, bad, undignified.
- The secularization of medicine: Separated from the values that once made it a service-oriented profession,

a calling, medicine has become more of a business, and people regard doctors as less caring than in the past.

• The interventionist mentality: We create more and more technology to deal with increasing problems. Instead of adjusting to accommodate maladapted conditions, we try to eliminate them.

• Functional assessment: Looking at people in terms of what they do and contribute to society as a measure of worth.[13]

Political analysts note that Americans are increasingly reluctant to pay for various social programs, including health care for the poor. This clashes with the notion that everyone deserves all available care, regardless of cost. Yet who would not want the best for themselves and their loved ones? Jeffrey Lyon concludes,

No matter what cost-containment schemes government adopts, it seems doubtful that runaway health care rates can be controlled without a fundamental change in consumer attitudes. . . . Most of us have come to regard top-of-the-line medical treatment as a fundamental right. We crave new discoveries that will extend our life span or improve our flawed bodies . . . but breakthrough treatments and revolutionary technologies come very dear. A Jarvik artificial heart transplant costs upwards of $250,000. A bone marrow transplant to cleanse the body of leukemia comes to $75,000. [The cost of an MRI scan] is $1,000, and the machine itself costs $1 million. In vitro fertilization may bring the joys of parenthood to childless couples, but it carries a price tag of $35,000. The bill for these immensely expensive items . . . is directly reflected in the national outlay for health.[14]

ACCESS TO HEALTH CARE

Despite the vast sums of money spent on health care, some Americans have had less access than others. Poverty, racism, a lack of caregivers and facilities in a given region, or lack of information or communication skills can all restrict access.

Does the government have a duty to provide health care for all citizens? Every industrialized nation except South Africa and the United States has a system of universal health insurance that covers everyone. These nations view health care as a human right. There are also practical considerations, since basic and preventive care may reduce the need for extensive, more costly care later on. But no one system is flawless; all seem to involve trade-offs of some kind. In certain countries, people may wait days to see a doctor, and there are waiting lists for elective surgery as well as lines at health clinics. People may travel longer distances for diagnostic tests, since advanced equipment is less prevalent.

For decades, Americans have wrestled with the question of what the government owes its citizens. In 1952, the President's Commission on the Health Needs of the Nation concluded, "access to the means for the attainment and preservation of health is a basic human right."[15] In 1964, as part of his War On Poverty, President Lyndon Johnson set up two government health insurance programs: Medicare for the elderly and Medicaid for the indigent. Community health centers were built in poor rural and urban areas. After 1964, the rate at which poor Americans used health care services increased by more than 20 percent; surgery rates rose about 40 percent.[16]

As of 1995, about thirty-seven million Americans (around 14 percent) still had no health insurance. Many were the working poor, too well off for Medicaid but unable to afford private insurance. Some areas also still lack doctors and health services. As a result, people may wait until they are so ill that they end up in an emergency room.

In 1982, The President's Commission for the Study of Ethical Problems in Medicine and Biomedical and Behavioral Research reiterated the idea that health care is a basic right, saying,

> Society has an ethical obligation to ensure equitable access to health care for all. The obligation rests on the special importance of health care, which derives from its role in relieving suffering, preventing premature death, restoring functioning, increasing opportunity, providing information about an individual's condition, and giving evidence of mutual empathy and compassion. . . . Although lifestyle and the environment can affect health status, differences in the need for health care are for the most part undeserved and not within an individual's control. . . . Equitable access to health care requires that all citizens be able to secure an adequate level of care without excessive burdens.[17]

The commission urged Americans to define an "adequate level of care—a floor below which no one ought to fall, not a ceiling above which no one may rise."[18] That "floor" need not entail all the care a person can get or might want, since this might create "impossible demands on society's resources for health care."[19]

The commission also said that costs should be distributed fairly among various parties—federal government, health care practitioners, institutions, and residents of different locations. Efforts to contain costs should not focus on limiting access of those people who are the least served, said the commission.

DEFINING "ACCESS" AND "EQUITY"

Americans have not yet reached a consensus about what a minimum, basic level of health care encompasses. Should access mean total equality for all citizens in regard to all health care? If not, which services are necessary? Which are not? Lists of important services have been developed by HMOs, which provide comprehensive health care to their members. Other people have suggested guidelines for developing such a list—for example, preventive measures that would improve a person's prospects for growth, such as maternal and child services. During health care debates in Congress, members have not agreed on a list of basic services needed for a decent, tolerable level of health.

Author Samuel Gorovitz offers some alternatives. First, the United States could develop a system with equal spending for each person. But some people rarely need care while others need a great deal. Or, second, the system could strive to give each individual equal health. This seems impossible, since individuals differ so greatly in their physical traits. Third, every person could have access to care up to some limit, which would be defined. Those who could afford more services could buy them.[20]

Fourth, people with similar conditions could be treated the same. Along with this, the nation might decide not to treat certain conditions at all. Health care analyst Amy Gutmann writes, "The most striking result of applying the equal access principle in the United States would be the creation of a one-class system of health care. Services and goods that meet health care needs would be equally available to everyone who was equally needy."[21] This system would not allow people with more money to buy preferred medical services that were not also equally accessible to the poor.

SETTING PRIORITIES

Many people question priorities in health care and other programs in America. For example, the Reagan administration passed regulations that required hospitals to save handicapped and defective newborns but asked Congress to cut federal funding for various social services.[22] Congress cut 25 percent of the Maternal and Child Health (MCH) budget, which funds prenatal care, genetic counseling and screening, treatment for birth defects and chronic childhood diseases, and programs for handicapped children.

Reagan also reduced funding for community health centers, where low-income women often receive care during pregnancy. Low birth weight and prematurity are linked with illness and handicaps and occur more often when pregnant women receive little care. Sara Rosenbaum, of the Children's Defense Fund, said,

> This country sees the trees but not the forest. We have . . . amazing lifesaving operations to save premature and sick babies. But we've not been energetic in investing in preventive services to avoid some of these tragedies. Prenatal care costs $1,500 counting routine medical visits and delivery. A complete food package for pregnant women costs $30 a month. But it costs $1,000 a day to grow a baby in an incubator. Would you rather grow a baby in his mother's stomach or an incubator?[23]

The 1993 Clinton Health Care Plan, developed by a panel headed by Hillary Rodham Clinton, addressed these issues and proposed more preventive care, such as childhood immunizations and programs to promote early diagnosis and treatment. The Clinton plan also mandated universal insurance coverage, mostly through employers, the basis of the current insurance program. However, the plan was attacked by insurance companies and various other groups, politicians, and individuals. Critics said the plan was too complicated and involved "too much government" in health care.

As of 1995, no major health care reform bill had been passed, and the debate over spending and priorities goes on. Posing some hard questions, ethicist B. D. Colen asks, "Do we really want to [spend upward of $2 billion a year] saving pound-and-a-half babies in an era when we are cutting back on childhood immunization and school lunch programs? Should we be spending an average of $140,000 per baby for neonatal intensive care when about 15 percent of the survivors will suffer from defects of one kind or another? These are easy questions to duck. They are not easy questions to answer."[24]

A 1993 case fueled the debate over costs and benefits. The Lakeberg family of Pennsylvania had Siamese twins who shared a single liver and heart. Doctors said there was only a 1 percent chance even one child would survive. The parents decided on a complicated operation to separate the twins, during which one baby would have to die so that the other might have a chance. The surgery and other medical and hospital costs were about $1.3 million, publicly financed, since the family had no insurance.

The twin named Amy died during the surgery while Angela survived. But Angela, too, died a year later. Although commentators sympathized with the family's plight, they again questioned whether so much money should be spent when survival is remote. Yet, as John Driscoll, a physician at Columbia-Presbyterian Medical Center, says, "I don't think Americans are ready to be told, 'Sorry. Nobody will pay for your baby. It's too costly.'"[25]

The state of Oregon addressed these hard questions in the early 1990s, developing a list of things they would not fund, including lower back pain care and treatment for advanced cases of AIDS. The state said there would be no more publicly funded transplants until people living below the poverty line had basic health care. Criticism mounted as an Oregon man died because he did not receive funding for his transplant.

Public policy expert Richard Lamm noted that California voted to fund such transplants while choosing to eliminate 270,000 low-income people from its Medicaid program. More people died or will die as a result of this decision than would die from not receiving transplants, says Lamm.[26]

The idea of limiting care—rationing—upsets many people. Critics ask why we should limit health care, since Americans also spend billions of dollars on sports, leisure activities, luxury items, alcoholic beverages, cigarettes, cosmetics, and national defense. Yet there is no guarantee that money can be siphoned from these things to pay for health care.

Decisions about allocating health care dollars are value-laden. How much should go to prevention versus treatment? How much for today's citizens versus research to help people in the future? How much for the elderly versus young people? What about non-life-threatening surgery? High-tech diagnostic tests? Consultants who are specialists?

Should people who abuse their health or ignore medical advice be treated like those who are careful? Some people would like a system that refused to pay for health problems viewed as self-inflicted—for example, lung cancer in smokers, liver disease in alcoholics. But how far can this idea be extended—to IV drug users with AIDS? Obese people with heart problems?

In 1995, Congress considered major cuts in the Medicare program for the elderly. Statistics show that restricting care for the elderly would not save much money. Dr. Ezekiel Emanuel, a Harvard ethicist, says that 70 percent of dying people already forgo heroic medical care and die at home. If all died at home, it would save just 3.3 percent of the health care bill.[27]

Should public money fund fertility treatments? In California, through the Medicaid program, a woman received fertility drugs and gave birth to seven infants, all very premature and in need of intensive care. When those receiving public assistance have more children, they need more support. People in this situation have argued that they have a right to any health care that would be available to others who were not poor. They claim the government cannot restrict their "reproductive rights." Other sticky questions arise: If the government is paying the cost, should it be able to tell certain families with genetic diseases not to have children?

Richard D. Lamm, director of the Center for Public Policy and Contemporary Issues at the University of Colorado in Denver, is one who believes that "public funds should buy the most health for the most people. As we cease to think of health care as a market commodity and start to think of it as a community resource, many allocation questions will be asked and new ways of ethical thinking will emerge."[28] Lamm believes that America has paid a high price for focusing on individuals instead of the larger society. He says,

> A community hospital in Europe serves the community; it has a geographic accountability, while a community hospital in the United States (with few exceptions) looks only at patients who walk in the door. We obsess about individual cases, but ignore the failure of the system that surrounds us. . . . We must recognize that the ultimate ethical question is not how to give all the 'beneficial' medicine to each individual but how to maximize the health of the community.[29]

In Great Britain, for instance, treatment is withheld from some babies with myelomeningocele who are thought to have a poor prognosis. Kidney dialysis may be denied to people over age fifty-five. Infants born weighing under 1.64 pounds are unlikely to receive intensive care. However, there are comprehensive, widespread, and compassionate services for the handicapped and their families.[30]

Should the United States move toward a system more like the one in Great Britain? In that kind of system, the welfare of the larger society may take precedence over individual desires. People may have fewer choices about their doctors and the type of health care they receive and may have to put up with some inconveniences, such as longer waits for nonemergency care. On the other hand, everyone has access to basic health care, and the nation spends less of its gross national product on health care than the United States.

TOUGH CHOICES AHEAD

In the future, wrenching questions may have to be confronted as even the wealthiest nations have difficulty meeting the demand for scarce medical resources, says Jeffrey Lyon.[31] There is no perfect solution. As one person or group gains, another loses.

Says economic analyst Robert J. Samuelson, "Science constantly expands the reach of health care, but what's socially useful and what isn't? We know we can't afford everything for everyone; but neither do we want to deny anything to anyone." Yet Americans must deal with these "messy questions." Says Samuelson: "If health spending continues its rapid advance, it could reach 30 percent of national income by 2030. This almost certainly won't happen, because at some point we will find it intolerable."[32]

Daniel Callahan suggests, "We should give much higher priority to making people comfortable than to things that save lives and cure people. . . . Those will be painful choices, but if we continue to hide them, we will never make them wisely."[33] Author Andrew Kimbrell states the problem this way: "We have a poor history of controlling technology. We have to ask: 'What is progress for us?' and then pick technologies that fit that vision of progress."[34]

More and more, we will confront these health-planning issues as we decide whether a new hospital should be built or a local hospital should add new beds, how much money will be spent and on what, and what kinds of environmental and other safety standards are important for health. As citizens, we will exercise our judgment at the ballot box, at civic meetings, while serving on committees, and perhaps in our jobs. As the limits of medicine continue to be stretched, there will be more uncharted territory, more choices to be made. These require a careful consideration of rights and responsibilities, resources and limits.

Bioethical questions are infinitely compelling because they deal with the nature of humans and how we define life itself. They evoke deep hopes and fears about life and death. The answers that we develop to these questions will determine if we use our expanding knowledge well and apply the wonders of science in a way that enhances the well-being of individuals and of our nation.

SOURCE NOTES

ONE

1. Jane J. Stein, *Making Medical Choices: Who Is Responsible?* (Boston: Houghton Mifflin, 1978), 11.

2. Helga Kuhse, "An Ethical Approach to IVF and ET: What Ethics Is All About," in William Walters and Peter Singer, eds. *Test Tube Babies* (Melbourne, Australia: Oxford University Press, 1982), 24.

3. Joseph Fletcher, *Humanhood: Essays in Biomedical Ethics* (Buffalo, New York: Prometheus, 1979), 116.

4. Kathy A. Fackelmann, "DNA Dilemmas: Readers and 'experts' weigh in on biomedical ethics," *Science News*, December 17, 1994, 408.

5. *Making Health Care Decisions: The Ethical and Legal Implications of Informed Consent in the Patient-Practitioner Relationship. Volume Two: Appendices, Empirical Studies of Informed Consent* (Washington, D.C.: U.S. Government Printing Office, 1982), 56.

6. The President's Commission for the Study of Ethical Problems in Medicine and Biomedical and Behavioral Research. *Securing Access to Health Care* (Washington, D.C.: U.S. Government Printing Office, 1982), 1.

7. Kenneth Vaux, *Biomedical Ethics: Morality for the New Medicine* (New York: Harper and Row, 1974), 53.

8. Fletcher, *Humanhood*, 8.

TWO

1. Quoted in B. D. Colen, *Hard Choices: Mixed Blessings of Modern Medical Technology* (New York: Putnam, 1986), 65.

125

2. "Concerns Agree To Halt Push Of Hormones," *New York Times*, October 7, 1994, A23.

3. Rudy Larini, "Garden's Designer Genes," *Sunday Star Ledger* (New Jersey), August 29, 1993, 8.

4. Quoted in Gerald Snyder, *Test Tube Life: Scientific Advance and Moral Dilemma* (New York: Julian Messner, 1982), 119.

5. Ibid., 121.

6. Ibid., 97.

7. Quoted in Tim Friend, "How Scientists Came to Take Step Toward Cloning Humans," *USA Today*, November 2, 1993.

8. John A. Robertson, "The Question of Human Cloning," *Hastings Center Report*, March–April 1994, 7. 6–14.

9. Robert F. Weaver, "Changing Life's Genetic Blueprint," *National Geographic*, December 1984, 829–831.

10. Quoted in Kitta MacPherson, " 'State' of Biotechnology," *Sunday Star Ledger* (Union County, New Jersey), April 3, 1994, 10.

11. Colen, *Hard Choices*, 64.

12. Richard Liebmann-Smith, "It's a Boy (Blond-Haired, Blue-Eyed, Even-Tempered, Ivy-Bound)," *New York Times Magazine*, February 7, 1993, 21.

13. David Suzuki and Peter Knudtson, *Genethics: The Clash Between the New Genetics and Human Values* (Cambridge, Mass.: Harvard University Press, 1989), 14.

THREE

1. Gina Kolata, "Tests to Assess Risks for Cancer Raising Questions," *New York Times*, March 27, 1995, A9.

2. Jane J. Stein, *Making Medical Choices: Who Is Responsible?* (Boston: Houghton Mifflin, 1978), 77.

3. Kolata, "Tests," A9.

4. Quoted in Stein, *Making Medical Choices*, 54.

5. Ibid.

6. Kolata, "Tests," A1.

7. Ibid., A9.

8. Ibid.

9. Mike Snider, "How Genetics Can Be Used Against You," *USA Today*, November 17, 1993, 9D.

10. "Hostage to Our Genes?" *New York Times*, September 22, 1994, A27.

11. Ibid.

12. Quoted in Snider, "How Genetics Can Be Used Against You," 9D.

13. Ibid.

14. Quoted in Warren E. Leary, "Using Gene Tests to Deny Jobs Is Ruled Illegal," *New York Times*, April 8, 1995.

15. William Daniel, "Human Life of Embryo Is Common Sense," in William Walters and Peter Singer, eds. *Test Tube Babies* (Melbourne, Australia: Oxford University Press, 1982), 48.

16. Thomas Shannon, *Bioethics* (Ramsey, N.J.: The Paulist Press, 1981), 23.

17. See Supreme Court case: *In re Cavitt*, 192 Neb. 712, 715; 157 N.W. 2nd 171, 175 (1968).

18. "Fertile Ground," *Scientific American*, February 1994, 26.

19. Quoted in Annette Fuentes, "The Selling of Humanity," *New York Daily News*, January 10, 1994.

20. Quoted in A. Rosenfeld, *The Second Genesis: The Coming Control of Life* (Englewood Cliffs, N.J.: Prentice Hall, 1969), 145.

21. Gina Kolata, "Should Children Be Told If Genes Predict Illness?" *New York Times*, September 26, 1994, A1, A14.

22. Ibid, A14.

23. Ibid.

24. Ibid.

FOUR

1. Rick Bragg, "Cheating Death, and Testing a Reproductive Law," *New York Times*, December 22, 1994, A16.

2. Quoted in Gina Kolata, "Fetal Ovary Transplant Is Envisioned," *New York Times*, January 6, 1994, A16.

3. Ibid.

4. Ibid.

5. B. D. Colen, *Hard Choices: Mixed Blessings of Modern Medical Technology* (New York: Putnam, 1986), 92.

6. Seth Mydans, "Fertility Clinic Told to Close Amid Complaints," *New York Times*, May 29, 1995, 7.

7. Ibid.

8. Pope Pius XII, Address to the Fourth International Congress of Catholic Doctors, September 29, 1949, quoted in Gerald Snyder, *Test Tube Life: Scientific Advance and Moral Dilemma* (New York: Julian Messner, 1982), 116.

9. Quoted in Jane Perlez, "Warsaw Bans a Clinic's In Vitro Fertilization Treatments," *New York Times*, March 19, 1995, A9.

10. Leon Kass, "Babies by Means of *In Vitro* Fertilization: Unethical Experiments on the Unborn?" *New England Journal of Medicine*, November 18, 1971, 1177.

11. "Cost of Test Tube Babies Averages $72,000," *New York Times*, July 28, 1994, A16.

12. Paul Ramsey, "Shall We 'Reproduce'?" *Journal of the American Medical Association*, June 12, 1972, 1482.

13. Gerald Snyder, *Test Tube Life*, 58.

14. Samuel Gorovitz, *Doctors' Dilemmas* (New York: Macmillan, 1982), 169.

15. Sir Frank Little, "Test Tube Baby Research Involves Moral Questions," in William Walters and Peter Singer, eds. *Test Tube Babies* (Melbourne, Australia: Oxford University Press, 1982), 40.

16. Quoted in "Frozen Embryos' Fate Awaits L.I. Custody Battle," *New York Times*, June 25, 1994, A1.

17. Ibid.

18. Ibid.

19. Quoted in Bonnie Steinbock and Ron McClamrock, "When Is Birth Unfair to the Child?" *Hastings Center Report*, November–December 1994, 21.

20. Ibid.

21. Susan Chira, "Of a Certain Age, and in a Family Way," *New York Times*, January 2, 1994, D5.

22. John Tagliabue, "In Italy, a Child Is Born and So Is a Lively Debate," *New York Times International*, January 13, 1995, A8.

23. "Newlywed Hopes to Use Sperm of Dead Spouse to Start a Family," *New York Times*, June 5, 1994, A34.

24. Bragg, "Cheating Death," A16.

25. Quoted in "Ruling Left Intact in Sperm Bequest," *New York Times*, September 5, 1993, A36.

26. Jane J. Stein, *Making Medical Choices: Who Is Responsible?* (Boston: Houghton Mifflin, 1978), 63.

27. "New Chinese Law Prohibits Sex-Screening of Fetuses," *New York Times*, November 15, 1994, A5.

28. Clifford Grobstein, *Science and the Unborn* (New York: Basic, 1988), 90–91.

29. Michael Novak, "Another Look at 'Baby M.': Buying and Selling Babies, Limitations on the Marketplace." *Commonweal*, July 17, 1987, 406.

30. Gerald F. Kreyche, "Surrogate Motherhood: An Ethical and Moral Dilemma," *USA Today*, November 21, 1987, 67.

31. Tamar Lewin, "Man Accused of Killing Son Borne By Surrogate Mother," *New York Times*, January 19, 1995, A16.

32. Ibid.

FIVE

1. Bette-Jane Crigger, ed. *Cases in Bioethics: Selections from the Hastings Center Reports* (New York: St. Martin's Press, 1993), 149.

2. Joseph Fletcher, *Humanhood: Essays in Biomedical Ethics* (Buffalo, New York: Prometheus, 1979), 178–179.

3. Quoted in Kenneth Vaux, *Biomedical Ethics: Morality for the New Medicine* (New York: Harper and Row, 1974), 29–30.

4. *Making Health Care Decisions: The Ethical and Legal Implications of Informed Consent in the Patient-Practitioner Relationship.* Volume One: Appendices, Empirical Studies of Informed Consent. Washington, D.C.: U.S. Government Printing Office, 2–3.

5. From a study by Robert A. Hahn, quoted in *Making Health Care Decisions: The Ethical and Legal Implications of Informed Consent in the Patient-Practitioner Relationship.* Vol. Three, Appendix F. (Washington, D.C.: U.S. Government Printing Office, 1982), 1.

6. Quoted in "U.S. Promises to Release Data on Plutonium Tests," *New York Times*, November 21, 1993, A30.

7. Philip M. Boffey, "Should We Make Research Embryos?" *New York Times*, November 25, 1994, A36.

8. Congregation for the Doctrine of Faith. *Instruction on Respect for Human Life in Its Origin and the Dignity of Procreation: Replies to Certain Questions of the Day* (Vatican City: Vatican Polyglot Press, 1987), 16–18. Quoted in Grobstein, *Science and the Unborn*, 96.

9. W. E. May, *Human Existence, Medicine, and Ethics* (Chicago: Franciscan Herald Press, 1977), 21.

10. Fletcher, *Humanhood*, 104.

11. Quoted in Natalie Angier, "Rules Due on Disputed Embryo Research," *New York Times*, September 6, 1994, C10.

12. Ibid.

13. Andrea Rock, "The Breast Cancer Experiment," *Ladies' Home Journal*, February 1995, 144ff.

14. Charles Weijer, "Our Bodies, Our Science," *The Sciences*, May/June 1995, 43.

15. Quoted in Gina Kolata, "Hospitals Use Bodies of Dead for Practice," *New York Times*, December 15, 1994, A22.

SIX

1. Carl Greiner, "Ethical Issues in Organ Transplantation: Who Is In the Circle?" *The Key Reporter*, Summer 1993, 7.

2. Gorovitz, *Doctor's Dilemma*, 185.

3. Greiner, "Ethical Issues in Organ Transplantation: Who Is In the Circle?" 6.

4. Ibid.

5. Ibid., 8–9.

6. Linda C. Fentiman, "Organ Donations: The Failure of Altruism," *Issues in Science and Technology*, Fall 1994, 43–48.

7. Tim Friend, "Living Secrets of Fetal Tissue," *USA Today, Science Today*, May 18, 1993, 1.

8. Kathy A. Fackelmann, "Study Sizes Up Fetal Cells for Transplant," *Science News*, January 7, 1995, 6.

9. Ibid.

10. Jeffrey Paul, "A Prisoner in Need of a Bone Marrow Transplant," in Crigger, ed. *Cases in Bioethics*, 270.

11. Paul T. Menzel, "Rescuing Lives: Can't We Count," *Hastings Center Report*, January–February, 1994, 22.

12. Ibid., 23.

13. "In Organ Transplants, America First?" in *Cases in Bioethics*, 252.

14. Ibid., 254.

SEVEN

1. Joseph Fletcher, *Humanhood: Essays in Biomedical Ethics* (Buffalo, New York: Prometheus, 1979), 164.

2. The President's Commission for the Study of Ethical Problems in Medicine and Biomedical and Behavioral Research. *Summing Up*. (Washington, D.C.: U.S. Government Printing Office, 1982), 31.

3. B. D. Colen, *Hard Choices: Mixed Blessings of Modern Medical Technology* (New York: Putnam, 1986), 119.

4. Jeffrey Lyon, *Playing God in the Nursery*, (New York: Norton, 1986), 60.

5. Grobstein, *Science and the Unborn*, 114–115.

6. Quoted in Jane J. Stein, *Making Medical Choices: Who Is Responsible?* (Boston: Houghton Mifflin, 1978), 112–113.

7. Lyon, *Playing God in the Nursery*, 115.

8. Ibid.

9. T. Morgenthau, "The Case of Baby Jane Doe, Continued," *Newsweek*, December 1983, 37.

10. Lyon, *Playing God in the Nursery*, 115.

11. Ibid., 11.

12. Ibid., 125–126.

13. Ibid., 200.

14. Ibid., 69.

15. Ibid., 337.

16. Ibid., 125.

17. Ibid., 337

18. Lisa Belkin, "He Lived, Who Pays?" *New York Times Magazine*, January 31, 1993, 58.

EIGHT

1. *Cruzan v. Director, Missouri Department of Health*. 497 U.S. 261

2. Jeffrey Lyon, *Playing God in the Nursery*, (New York: Norton, 1986), 208.

3. Joseph Fletcher, *Humanhood: Essays in Biomedical Ethics* (Buffalo, New York: Prometheus, 1979), 150.

4. The President's Commission for the Study of Ethical Problems in Medicine and Biomedical and Behavioral Research. *Summing Up*. (Washington, D.C.: U.S. Government Printing Office, 1982), 34.

5. Lyon, *Playing God in the Nursery*, 66.

6. Quoted in Gail B. Slap, M.D. and Martha M. Jablow, "Debating Rights of the Young to Say No to Medical Care," *New York Times*, November 10, 1994, C10.

7. "Girl Flees After Clash of Cultures On Illness," *New York Times*, November 12, 1994, 6.

8. B. D. Colen, *Hard Choices: Mixed Blessings of Modern Medical Technology* (New York: Putnam, 1986), 252–253.

9. Daniel Callahan, *Setting Limits: Medical Goals in an Aging Society* (New York: Simon and Schuster, 1987), throughout text.

10. "What Do We Owe the Elderly?" *Hastings Center Report*, March–April, 1994, S11.

11. "Suicide Proposal Would Permit Prescriptions for Deadly Drugs," *New York Times*, October 16, 1994, A1.

12. Robert A. Burt, "Death Made Too Easy," *New York Times*, November 16, 1994, Op-Ed.

13. "Death and Dying: The Final Chapter," *Harvard Health Letter* February 1995, 1–3.

14. B. D. Colen, *Hard Choices: Mixed Blessings of Modern Medical Technology* (New York: Putnam, 1986), 263.

15. Interviewed in "In the Name of the Child," *Dateline NBC*, March 14, 1994.

16. Gina Kolata, "Withholding Care From Patients: Boston Case Asks Who Decides," *New York Times*, April 3, 1995, A1.

17. Ibid. B8.

18. "Readers Health Forum," *Newsweek*, September 19, 1994, 16.

NINE

1. B. D. Colen, *Hard Choices: Mixed Blessings of Modern Medical Technology* (New York: Putnam, 1986), 24.

2. Jeffrey Lyon, *Playing God in the Nursery*, (New York: Norton, 1986), 283.

3. Colen, *Hard Choices: Mixed Blessings of Modern Medical Technology*, 25; Lyon, *Playing God in the Nursery*, 290.

4. Ibid., 252–253.

5. Richard Lamm, "Who Pays for AZT?" in *Cases in Bioethics*, 282.

6. Quoted in Colen, *Hard Choices*, 15.

7. Michael Meyer and Andrew Murr, "Not My Health Care," *Newsweek*, January 10, 1994, 36.

8. Richard A. McCormick, "Value Variables in the Health-Care Reform Debate," *America*, May 29, 1993, 8.

9. Ibid.

10. Ibid. 8–9.

11. Ibid., 9–10.

12. Ibid., 10.

13. Ibid., 13.

14. Lyon, *Playing God in the Nursery*, 282–283:

15. *The President's Commission on the Health Needs of the Nation* (Washington, D.C.: U.S. Government Printing Office, 1953), 3.

16. Karen Davis and Cathy Schoen, *Health and the War on Poverty: A Ten Year Appraisal*. Washington, D.C.: Brookings Institution, 1978), 41–48.

17. The President's Commission for the Study of Ethical Problems in Medicine and Biomedical and Behavioral Research. *Summing Up.* (Washington, D.C.: U.S. Government Printing Office, 1982), 29.

18. Ibid., 30.

19. Ibid.

20. Gorovitz, *Doctor's Dilemma*, 181–182.

21. Amy Gutmann, "For and Against Equal Access to Health Care," in *Securing Access to Health Care*, vol. 2, 53.

22. Quoted in Lyon, *Playing God in the Nursery*, 267.

23. Ibid., 259.

24. Colen, *Hard Choices*, 23.

25. Melinda Beck, et al."Rationing Health Care," *Newsweek*, June 27, 1994, 35.

26. Richard D. Lamm, "The Ethics of Excess," *The Hastings Center Report*, November December 1994, 14.

27. Beck, "Rationing Health Care," 36.

28. Lamm, "The Ethics of Excess," 14.

29. Ibid.

30. Lyon, *Playing God in the Nursery*, 288.

31. Ibid.

32. Robert J. Samuelson, "Will Reform Bankrupt Us?" *Newsweek*, August 15, 1994, 54.

33. Beck, "Rationing Health Care," 36.

34. Andrew Kimbrell, *The Human Body Shop*, New York: Harper-Collins, 1994, 298.

FURTHER READING

The following titles are in addition to those listed in the Source Notes.

BOOKS

Aaron, Henry J., and William B. Schwartz. *The Painful Prescription: Rationing Hospital Care*. Washington, D.C.: Brookings Institution, 1984.

Aday, L. A. et al. *Health Care in the U.S.: Equitable for Whom?* Beverly Hills: Sage, 1980.

Arras, John, and Nancy K. Rhoden, eds. *Ethical Issues in Modern Medicine*. 3d ed. Mountain View, Cal.: Mayfield, 1989.

Barry, Vincent E. *Moral Aspects of Health Care*. Belmont, Cal.: Wadsworth, 1982.

Bayles, Michael D. *Reproductive Ethics*. Englewood Cliffs, N.J.: Prentice Hall, 1984.

Bendick, Jeanne. *Super People: Who Will They Be?* New York: McGraw Hill, 1980.

Callahan, Daniel. *What Kind of Life? The Limits of Medical Progress*. New York: Simon and Schuster, 1990.

Callahan, Daniel, and Sissela Bok, eds. *Ethics Teaching in Higher Education*. New York: Plenum Press, 1980.

Cook-Deegan, Robert. *The Gene Wars: Science, Politics, and the Human Genome*. New York: Norton, 1994.

Draper, Elaine. *Risky Business: Genetic Testing and Exclusionary Practices in the Hazardous Workplace.* New York: Cambridge University Press, 1991.

Dudley, William, ed. *Death and Dying: Opposing Viewpoints.* San Diego: Greenhaven, 1992.

Feinberg, Joel. *Harm to Others.* New York: Oxford University Press, 1984.

Gaylin, Willard M., and Ruth Macklin, eds. *Who Speaks for the Child? The Problem of Proxy Consent.* New York: Plenum Press, 1982.

Gostin, Larry, ed. *Surrogate Motherhood: Politics and Privacy.* Bloomington, Ind.: University of Indiana Press, 1990.

Harron, Frank, et al. *Health and Human Values.* New Haven, Conn.: Yale University Press, 1983.

The Hastings Center. *Guidelines for the Termination of Life-Sustaining Treatment.* Bloomington, Ind.: University of Indiana Press, 1988.

Hawke, Nigel. *Genetic Engineering 1991.* New York: Gloucester, 1991.

Jones, James H. *Bad Blood: The Tuskegee Syphilis Experiment,* 2d ed. New York: Free Press, 1992.

Knox, Jean. *Death and Dying.* New York: Chelsea House, 1989.

Kuhse, Helga, and Peter Singer. *Should the Baby Live? The Problems of Handicapped Newborns.* New York: Oxford University Press, 1985.

Levine, Robert J. *Ethics and Regulation of Clinical Research,* 2d ed. New Haven: Yale University Press, 1988.

Lynn, Joanne, ed. *No Extraordinary Means: The Choice to Forgo Life-Sustaining Food and Water.* Bloomington, Ind.: University of Indiana Press, 1986.

McCartney, Scott. *Defying the Gods: Inside the New Frontiers of Organ Transplants.* New York: Macmillan, 1994.

McNeil, Paul M. *The Ethics and Politics of Human Experimentation.* Cambridge, England: Cambridge University Press, 1993.

Mabie, Margot C. *Bioethics and the New Medical Technology.* New York: Atheneum, 1993.

Madison, Arnold. *Transplanted and Artificial Body Organs.* New York: Beaufort, 1981.

Menzel, Paul T. *Strong Medicine: The Ethical Rationing of Health Care.* New York: Oxford University Press, 1990.

New York Task Force on Life and the Law. *When Others Must Choose: Deciding for Patients Without Capacity.* New York: N.Y.S. Task Force, 1992.

Office of Technology Assessment, Congress of the United States. *Biomedical Ethics in U.S. Public Policy.* Washington, D.C.: U.S. Government Printing Office, 1993.

O'Neill, Terry, ed. *Biomedical Ethics.* Westport, Conn.: Greenwood Press, 1994.

Pollack, Robert. *Signs of Life: The Language and Meaning of DNA.* Boston: Houghton Mifflin, 1994.

President's Commission for the Study of Ethical Problems in Medicine and Biological and Behavioral Research. *Compensating Research Injury* (1982); *Deciding to Forgo Life-sustaining Treatment* (1983); *Defining Death* (1981); *Implementing Human Research Regulations* (1983); *Protecting Human Subjects* (1981); *Screening and Counseling for Genetic Conditions* (1983); *Securing Access to Health Care* (1983); *Splicing Life* (1982); *Summing Up* (1983); *Whistleblowing in Biomedical Research* (1982), (Washington, D.C.: U.S. Government Printing Office).

Rachels, James S. *The End of Life: Euthanasia and Morality.* New York: Oxford University Press, 1986.

Rostand, Jean. *Humanly Possible.* New York: Saturday Review Press, 1973.

Simmons, Roberta G. et al. *Gift of Life: The Social and Psychological Impact of Organ Transplantation.* New York: John Wiley, 1977.

Weil, William B., Jr., and Martin Benjamin, eds. *Ethical Issues at the Onset of Life.* Boston: Blackwell Scientific Publications, 1987.

Weiss, Ann E. *Bioethics: Dilemmas in Modern Medicine.* Springfield, N.J.: Enslow, 1985.

Wilkie, Tom. *Perilous Knowledge: The Human Genome Project and Its Implications.* Berkeley: University of California Press, 1994.

PERIODICALS

"The Ambiguity of Organ Transplants," *The Christian Century*, April 2, 1980.

Angier, Natalie. "Biologists Find Key Genes That Shape Patterning of Embryos," *New York Times*, January 11, 1994, C1, C13.

———. "Gene Experiment Offers Insight Into the Basis of Childhood Cancer," *New York Times*, August 31, 1993, C4.

———. "Gene Experiment to Reverse Inherited Disease Is Working," *New York Times*, April 1, 1994, A1, A16.

———. "Rules Due on Disputed Embryo Research," *New York Times*, September 6, 1994, C1, C10.

———. "With New Fly, Science Outdoes Hollywood," *New York Times*, March 24, 1995, A1, A15.

Begley, Sharon, and Adam Rogers. "It's All in the Genes," *Newsweek*, September 5, 1994, 64.

Blumstein, James F. "Federal Organ Transplantation Policy: A Time for Reassessment?" *University of California at Davis Law Review*, 22 (1989), 451–497.

Bragg, Rick. "Cheating Death, and Testing a Reproductive Law," *New York Times*, December 22, 1994, A16.

Broome, John. "Fairness Versus Doing the Most Good," *Hastings Center Report*, July–August 1994, 36–39.

Burt, Robert A., "Death Made Too Easy," *New York Times*, November 16, 1994, Op-Ed.

Capron, Alexander Morgan. "Grandma? No, I'm the Mother," *Hastings Center Report*, March–April 1994, 24.

"Cost of Test Tube Babies Averages $72,000," *New York Times*, July 28, 1994, A16.

"Death and Dying: The Final Chapter," *Harvard Health Letter* February 1995, 1–3.

Dworkin, Ronald. "When Is It Right to Die?" *New York Times*, May 17, 1994, A19.

Fackelmann, Kathy A. "Cloning Human Embryos," *Science News*, February 5, 1994, 92–95.

Fentiman, Linda C. "Organ Donations: The Failure of Altruism," *Issues in Science and Technology*, Fall 1994, 43–48.

Fitzgerald, Beth. "Jersey Lab Splices Veggie Gene," *Sunday Star Ledger* July 4, 1993, 4–6.

Franklin-Barbahosa, Cassandra. "DNA Profiling: The New Science of Identity," *National Geographic*, May 1992, 112–124.

"The High Cost of Having Some Babies," *Science News*, August 6, 1994, 95.

Hilchey, Tim. "Genetic Therapy Found for Dystrophy in Mice," *New York Times*, August 31, 1993, C3.

Hoversten, Paul. "Fetuses, Stillborn Were Part of Radiation Tests," *USA Today*, June 28, 1994, 1.

"How Far Should We Push Mother Nature?" *Newsweek*, January 17, 1994, 56.

Jennings, Bruce et al. "Ethical Challenges of Chronic Illness," *Hastings Center Report*, February/March 1988, 1–16.

Kass, Leon. "Babies by Means of *In Vitro* Fertilization: Unethical Experiments on the Unborn?" *New England Journal of Medicine*, November 18, 1971, 1177.

Kolata, Gina. "Advisory Panel Clears Way for Trying Genetic Therapy on Cardiovascular Disease," *New York Times*, September 14, 1994, B8.

———. "Battle Over a Baby's Future Raises Hard Ethical Issues," *New York Times*, December 27, 1994, A1, A12.

———. "Fetal Ovary Transplant Is Envisioned," *New York Times*, January 6, 1994, 1.

———. "Gene Technique Can Shape Future Generations," *New York Times*, November 22, 1994, C1, C10.

Lamm, Richard D. "The Ethics of Excess," *Hastings Center Report*, November–December 1994, 14–22.

Lewin, Tamar. "Man Accused of Killing Son Borne By Surrogate Mother," *New York Times*, January 19, 1995, A16.

McCormick, Richard A. "Value Variables in the Health-Care Reform Debate," *America*, May 29, 1993, 7–13.

Marshall, Eliot. "Political Fallout: A National Bioethics Board," *Science*, January 28, 1994, 473.

Merritt, Deborah Jones. "The Constitutional Balance Between Health and Liberty," *Hastings Center Report*, December 1986, 2–9.

Meyer, Michael, and Andrew Murr, "Not My Health Care," *Newsweek*, January 10, 1994, 36.

Miller, Julie Ann. "The Clergy Ponder the New Genetics," *Science News*, Vol. 125, March 24, 1984.

Morreim, E. Haavi. "Profoundly Diminished Life: The Casualties of Coercion," *Hastings Center Report*, January–February 1994, 33–42.

Novak, Michael. "Another Look at 'Baby M.': Buying and Selling Babies, Limitations on the Marketplace." *Commonweal*, July 17, 1987, 406–407.

Ramsey, Paul. "Manufacturing Our Offspring: Weighing the Risks," *Hastings Center Report*, October 1979, 9–13.

———. "Shall We 'Reproduce'?" *Journal of the American Medical Association*, June 12, 1972, 1482.

Reiser, Stanley Joel. "The Ethical Life of Health Care Organizations," *The Hastings Center Report*. November–December, 1994, 28–35.

"The Replacement Parts Dilemma: Who Should Give, Who Receive?" *Science Digest*, November, 1979.

Robertson, John A. "The Question of Human Cloning,"*Hastings Center Report*. March–April, 1994, 6–15.

Samuelson, Robert J. "Will [health care] Reform Bankrupt Us?" *Newsweek*, August 15, 1994, 50–54.

Serrill, Michael S. "Castration or Incarceration?" *Time*, December 12, 1983.

Snider, Mike. "How Genetics Can Be Used Against You," *USA Today*, November 17, 1993, 9D.

Steinbock, Bonnie, and Ron McClamrock, "When Is Birth Unfair to the Child?" *Hastings Center Report*, November–December 1994, 15–21.

"Suicide Proposal Would Permit Prescriptions for Deadly Drugs," *New York Times*, October 16, 1994, A1.

"Superkids?" *Time*, March 10, 1980.

"Twin Who Survived Separation Is Dead," *New York Times*, June 10, 1994, A18.

Wallis, Claudia. "Putting Lids on Medicare Costs," *Time*, October 10, 1983.

———. "The Stormy Legacy of Baby Doe," *Time* September 26, 1983.

Weijer, Charles. "Our Bodies, Our Science," *The Sciences*, May/June 1995, 41–45.

"What Do We Owe the Elderly?" *Hastings Center Report*, March–April 1994, S1–S12.

INDEX